SAY YES TO YOUR
Life

D0003827

DAILY MEDITATIONS
FOR ALCOHOLICS
AND ADDICTS

LEO BOOTH

Health Communications, Inc.
Deerfield Beach, Florida

www.hcibooks.com

Library of Congress Cataloging-in-Publication Data

Booth, Leo.

Say yes to your life : daily meditations for alcoholics and addicts / Leo Booth.

    p. cm.

  ISBN-13: 978-0-7573-0764-5 (trade paper)

  ISBN-10: 0-7573-0764-7 (trade paper)

  1. Recovering alcoholics—Prayers and devotions.   2. Recovering addicts—Prayers and devotions.   3. Devotional calendars.   I. Title.

BL625.9.A43.B66 2008

204'.32—dc22

                                       2008033962

Publisher: Health Communications, Inc.
               3201 S.W. 15th Street
               Deerfield Beach, FL 33442-8190

Cover photo ©PhotoDisc
Cover design by Larissa Hise Henoch
Interior design by Lawna Patterson Oldfield
Interior formatting by Dawn Von Strolley Grove

"*Each day's read is a spiritual gem.*"

—John Bradshaw, Author

"*I'm a recovering addict who happens to be Jewish, and I find a spiritual message on every page. A few readings lift an eyebrow, but those are the ones that stay with you.*"

—Dr. Michael Weiner, Ph.D., Addiction Researcher

"*The openness of the book reflects the openness of the author.*"

—Iman Jory Kareem, Therapist

"*A daily read that inspires faith and personal growth for inner healing. . . .*"

—Chic Bancroft, Interventionist

"*This book offers inspiring words of Love and Hope for those with or without an addiction.*"

—Dr. Valerie Watkins, Ph.D., Therapist

"*This book we give to all our clients. The insights, humor, and uplifting messages make it a welcome companion for everyone's life journey.*"

—Dr. Daniel Gatlin, Ph.D., Therapist

"*Reverend Leo's book is intriguing, fascinating, educational, and spiritual. He truly is an artist.*"

—Ed Storti, Interventionist

Also by Leo Booth
Say Yes to Your Spirit

Acknowledgments

The book *Say Yes to Life*, which has gone through three incarnations since it was originally published by HCI Books twenty years ago, is now presented as *Say Yes to Your Life* and it is even more powerful, reflecting an inclusive spirituality.

Writing a book and then seeing it "birthed" involves the professionalism of more than the author and it is important for me to express my gratitude to the following:

Kien Lam, who started working with me when I initially wrote *Say Yes to Life* twenty years ago, worked tirelessly with HCI to ensure that the corrections, updates, and artwork reflect the essence of *Say Yes to Your Life*.

Michele Matrisciani, who took the original manuscript and made the writing tighter and more vivid in expressing my thought pattern, so that each meditation was inclusive and gender sensitive. I began working with Michele on my new book *Say Yes to Your Spirit* in 2007 and she made the discipline of editing both exciting and creative.

I also want to thank the thousands of recovering people who over the years have shared stories and insights into spirituality that is really the foundation of this book *Say Yes to Your Life*. Thank you.

And lastly, Peter Vegso, Publisher and President of HCI, who loved the book twenty years ago and still loves it.

Affirm your spiritual *Yes*.

Introduction

When I wrote this book I was concerned that it should be inclusive, not representing any one religion or denomination, and open to every human being who desires to discover their God-given spirituality on a daily basis.

The 365 daily meditations throughout this book are personal, as they recount my personal struggle with a variety of topics, and because human beings are so similar, I have little doubt that you will be able, regardless of background, to identify with the feelings and struggles expressed within these pages.

Indeed, since its original publication twenty years ago, I have received hundreds of letters and emails from readers telling me how this book has saved their lives, given them hope, and allowed them to find a new understanding of spirituality throughout their recovery journey.

This book is not intended to convert people from their personal beliefs or convictions, but to show on a daily basis the connection between our lives as recovering people and the dynamic of spirituality.

This new and exciting edition of *Say Yes to Your Life* offers you help, hope, and empowerment.

Leo Booth

Spirituality

"It is not that I think or believe, but that I know."
Sir Arthur Conan Doyle

Some things I seem to know intuitively, and I know spirituality is involved in, and affects, everything. In a human being, it combines the physical, mental, and emotional states, but it also reaches beyond the human being and connects the peoples of the world. Spirituality is the force for good and wholeness in the universe.

This is not just an opinion or a thought. It is a feeling that runs so deep in my being that I know it must be true. When I read, listen to music, or watch a movie, this feeling is often evoked. I know God is alive in the world and wants it to be one.

In the silence of Your world I know You.

Martyrs

"A thing is not necessarily true because everyone dies for it."
Oscar Wilde

In the battle with alcoholism, my involvement with God's will for me is crucial. My choice is the result of God's gift of freedom, and freedom can be awfully real! The price of freedom is Auschwitz, the world's starving millions, and the dead drunk in a derelict building. People do insane and destructive things, usually because they think they know best. They die to protect their egos.

Today I am learning to detach spiritually to discover a pure and selfless love. I stand back and consider before I act. Often after a time of reflection, I see the event differently—and it is okay to change my mind.

*God, I understand choice is the key
to my humanity.*

Isolation

"No one is an island, entire of itself; everyone is a piece of the continent, a part of the main."
John Donne

For years, I thought I was alone—lost, isolated, and afraid. Today I understand this to be a symptom of my alcoholism, an aspect of my disease. Alcoholism is "cunning, baffling, and powerful." It is a mystery we have only begun to understand. One thing we know: The disease—the "ism" of alcoholism—involves more than the act of drinking. Feelings of inadequacy, isolation, and fear keep us from recovering until we discover the spiritual strength to confront the disease in our lives. The initial risk of letting go and trusting others is an essential part of the recovery process.

Dear God, I believe I am part of this world and an important part of You.

Freedom

"A hungry person is not a free person."
Adlai Stevenson

For years, I craved food. It was my escape from reality. It stopped the pain, loneliness, and anger for a moment. It felt good. Eventually, I began to feel bad, but I could not stop. I was addicted to sugar. My freedom was exchanged for doughnuts!

I heard someone talk about compulsion around cocaine and gambling. When I asked how he managed to abstain, he replied: "Talk about it, a day at a time!"

Today I am compulsive about getting well. I talk about my disease every day. The price of freedom is vulnerability. God is in the risk. I have taken it.

God, let me experience freedom
in the choices I make today.

Change

"It is the most unhappy people who most fear change."

Mignon McLaughlin

When I was drinking, I hated change. I hated things not being the same. I feared anything being different. Rarely did I want to go anywhere new. My attitudes were fixed and rigid. I resented any criticism of my behavior. The unexpected was seen as sabotage or a threat. My paranoia was extreme.

Today I have decided to let go of the control, the pretense, and the arrogance. I face life as it comes, and today I do not drink. I am responsible for my life, but I cannot control the world. I am learning to relax in the acceptance of my disease.

*May I always discover the courage
to change the things I can.*

Boredom

"Nothing is interesting if you are not interested."
Helen MacInnes

There is a distinction between "dry" and "sober." Sober alcoholics choose not to drink because they have accepted their alcoholism. Dry alcoholics are not drinking but are invariably angry and resentful and do not express these feelings. Their abstinence is not exciting because they are not interested in it; they are bored. They really want to drink. They have stopped drinking for reasons that do not include acceptance of the disease; thus, they are still victims of it.

Sobriety, by contrast, is an adventure into self. It greets the new day with enthusiasm and energy. Sobriety is the spiritual discovery of God in my life.

Let me always remember that my interests
in life reflect my interest in You.

God

*"I have had the experience of being gripped by
something stronger than myself, something people
call God."*
Carl Jung

God is beyond my comprehension. In a sense, we are all agnostics—none of us knows for certain, and uncertainty is part of faith. However, there are moments when God is vivid and alive in new and stimulating experiences that defy explanation except for saying "That's God."

Loving relationships, friendships, the beauty of nature, and the complexities of life and the universe, not to mention music, poetry, and the human conscience, all speak of God. History is full of holy people who carry the message that God is love and is to be discovered in my love of self and others.

*God, help me discover You
in my doubt and confusion.*

Miracles

"I haven't understood a bar of music in my life, but I have felt it."
Igor Stravinsky

A miracle is not meant to be understood but experienced. So much in life I will never understand. There is growth in confusion. I am not perfect. I will never be perfect. The mystery of life is exactly that it is a mystery.

As an alcoholic, I often sought to appear "as God." I had to have an answer for everything, even if I made up the answer! Not to know was humiliating for me because it took away control, my need to be in charge, my hopeless and exhausting quest for perfection. With failure to be perfect came the guilt, shame, and anger. Today I am able to live with life's daily confusions—and it's okay!

Great Spirit, help me never to lose touch
with the feelings that keep me human.

Extremists

"Extremists think 'communication' means agreeing with them."
Leo Rosten

As an alcoholic, I was an extremist. I was compulsive and obsessive about alcohol and about my opinions, thoughts, and attitude toward life. Anyone who disagreed with me was a fool! I only listened to those who said what I wanted to hear.

For years, the spiritual part of me was isolated and unhappy. Although I would never admit it, I was often wrong and in pain. I spent sleepless nights wondering how I could say I was sorry without apologizing! Today I appreciate those who have a different view of life. I can disagree without carrying a grudge. I can live with difference.

God, may I always hear what others are saying.

Difference

"The ways in which we express ourselves spiritually are beautiful and loving, creating unity and oneness."
Rob Eichberg

As a recovering alcoholic, I belong to a minority. As somebody with the disease of addiction, I am aware of my difference. I have experienced prejudice and injustice because I was not born like other people.

But in a spiritual sense, acceptance of my disease has given me a freedom that united me with other minorities, other "different" groups—the countless shades of humanity. My disease has produced a spiritual unity and bond with creation that make me rejoice in my difference and engender a tolerance of others that was not there before. In this sense, I thank God for my disease.

You who made the different also created the unity. Help me find both in my life.

Philosophy

"To teach us to live without certainty yet without being paralyzed by hesitation is perhaps the chief thing philosophy can do."
Bertrand Russell

I suppose the Twelve Steps are a practical philosophy for living positively with the disease of alcoholism: (a) Don't drink. (b) Find a God in your life that is understandable. (c) Begin to make positive choices in attitudes and behaviors. (d) Let "Never forget" be an essential part of the message.

The miracle of this philosophy is that it reaches out to so many who suffer with addictive compulsions and teaches us how to live with our imperfections. I believe the Twelve Steps are the answer to "The Fall" of humanity —we are going home to God.

Let me see beyond the logic
to Your loving energy.

Values

"The aim of education is the knowledge not of fact, but of values."
William R. Inge

Facts can confuse. They may be used as a façade or manipulated into lies. Facts are no substitute for human values.

Today I not only value my life—I value Life itself. When I walk in nature, I observe its beauty, experience its strength, and know I am a part of it all. My values have changed because I see myself as "part of" rather than "separate from." I belong to this planet, and what I do affects the essential value of life. With my respect for self comes a respect for property, people, cultures, and God.

What I truly value I do not pay for; what I cherish cannot be won or bought. Spirituality is free.

Teach me to value the richness of life.

Acceptance

"All things are woven together and the common bond is sacred . . . for they have been arranged together in their places and together make the same Universe."
Marcus Aurelius

I said I was a nonviolent drunk. Today I am able to see I was sarcastic and verbally violent, and this was no less painful or destructive to the victim. A target for my anger and venom was the faith and beliefs of others, especially when those differed radically from my own. My alcoholism made me a prejudiced and bigoted person, a prisoner of my arrogance.

My sobriety teaches me to be accepting and tolerant of the views and opinions of others. A spirituality that embraces everyone, rather than a narrow and restrictive religion, is my prescription for life. I have exchanged bigotry for freedom, and I am happy in God's world.

May my acceptance of others, regardless of culture or creed, lead to understanding.

Responsibility

"The fault is in us."
Hannah Arendt

As a drunk, I blamed everybody for my problems. My family was too controlling. I did not have people around who understood me. I worked too hard, and the people were too demanding. The weather was awful!

Today I accept my involvement with my past predicaments. Bad things happened to me because I created them in my life. This means good and creative things can also happen in my life if I create them. I need not remain the problem. I can be the solution!

Let me discover Your answer
in my response to life.

Popularity

"Few people are capable of expressing, with equanimity, opinions that differ from the prejudices of their social environment."
Albert Einstein

Part of my growth in sobriety is learning to say "No." For years, I tried to please everybody with the result that I pleased very few and became exhausted in the process! I have learned that sometimes I need to be unpopular to remain serene and practice my spiritual program.

To understand the gift of God's creation requires the acceptance that we are not the same and, as people, we will have different opinions and attitudes. Truth has many shades. To be unpopular at times is reality; truth is always real.

May I always say and do what I believe is right, regardless of public opinion.

Procrastination

"You cannot build a reputation on things you are going to do."
Mabel Newcomber

Procrastination is the addict's game. I will give up alcohol tomorrow. Soon, I will take an inventory of my eating habits. Later, I will express my anger and pain. Tomorrow and tomorrow—but it never happens!

The tragedy is that we not only bring pain and problems into our lives but we keep them there. Recovery requires action. Sobriety and the spiritual program demand movement.

God, may I talk openly about my pain today.

Creativity

"Creative intelligence in its various forms and activities is what makes humankind."
James Harvey Robinson

Spirituality means being positive and creative in all areas of my life. This I know to be true. I am part of God's love for the world. Through me, great and wonderful events unfold. Although I am not the Divine, I share God's Divinity. With this knowledge comes responsibility, because things only happen if I make them happen in my life. To simply know I am creative is not enough.

Today I work at my life like a carpenter works with wood. I chip away the things I do not want; I smooth the rough areas, and polish the things I want people to see. I accept responsibility for my creativity, and I thank God for it on a daily basis.

Teach me to use my life as a tool
for goodness, joy, and truth.

Gluttony

"Gluttony is not a secret vice."
Orson Welles

Food addiction—eating, forever dieting, starving—is the hidden disease that is becoming more obvious. But am I talking about it? Some recovering alcoholics minimize it and get lost in ice cream and doughnuts. For many, the pain around food is as real as alcohol or any other drug. The family and relationships suffer.

Today I am willing to talk about it. Spirituality affects all my life, and this involves my eating habits and body weight. God does not make junk, so I choose not to eat junk. Today I choose to talk about the buried emotions I am stuffing behind the food. That is a step toward living.

When I bless my food at mealtime,
may I also bless my abstinence.

Equality

*"Treat all persons alike. Give them all the same
laws. Give them all an even chance to live and
grow."*
Chief Joseph

Today it is important for me to remember that I am
not the only human being in the universe. I need to
respect and be considerate of others. Spirituality requires
that I treat all people with dignity and respect because
they carry something of God within them. The image
of God is with all people. In this way, I show and give
respect to self.

As an alcoholic, I was selfish and demanding, wanting my way all the time. Sobriety teaches me that "the
way" must include others; my fellow and sister humans
are part of my life and my journey. I cannot live in isolation and be sober.

*Spirit of the world, teach me to respect others
because, in this way, I respect myself.*

Belief

"One person with a belief is equal to a force of 99 who have only interest."
John Stuart Mill

I believe in sobriety because it works for me. It makes me feel good about myself. It has enabled me to rejoin the human race. I was tired of feeling lonely, ashamed, and isolated.

The belief I have in myself has rekindled a positive relationship with my higher power. Today God is a friend, and I understand more about what God wants for me. I am broad enough in my thinking to find God in everything positive and creative—from music to hugs!

Today I am able to face any pains or conflict. I know what it is to be a winner, and that does not mean I have to be perfect or in control.

Thank You for the gift of believing in myself.

Tolerance

"The price of freedom of religion or of speech or of the press is that we must put up with, and even pay for, a good deal of rubbish."
Justice Robert Jackson

I need to be tolerant in sobriety. I need to allow others to live according to their own standards and say what they feel.

Before, I was intolerant of people who were different. Much of what I criticized yesterday, I accept today; some things I still reject. To love someone does not require sameness; I can accept people without agreeing with what they say or how they behave.

Not everything I say or do is pure, and that has become my key to accepting others. My history teaches me that I benefit from the variety of opinions represented in humankind.

May I appreciate You
through the experiences of others.

Poetry

"Poetry is not an assertion of truth, but the making of that truth more fully real to us."
T. S. Eliot

God communicates in a thousand different ways, and one such way is poetry. Spirituality is discovering God in creation, and this involves far more than religion or denominationalism. Spirituality is a comprehensive approach to God's world and the unifying factor at the center of the universe. Spirituality is about what is true—wherever it is found in the world.

Poetry and other art forms become part of the spiritual journey for us as we struggle to understand and communicate Truth.

*In my enjoyment of poetry,
may I express my love for You.*

Sleep

"Sleep that knots up the raveled sleeve of care. . . ."
William Shakespeare

When I was new to recovery from alcoholism, I was told to remember the acronym HALT: Do not get too Hungry, Angry, Lonely, or Tired.

Sleep is something my body needs. Even if I do not always know it, my body does. The tiredness in my body is telling me to slow down. Sleep is part of my spiritual program because it enables me to feel rested, invigorated, and alive. Through sleep, I am able to be creative and positive in my life and show a practical love toward my body. Sleep is one way I take care of myself!

Thank You for the joy and rest
that come with sleep.

Opportunity

"Too many people are thinking of security instead of opportunity; they seem more afraid of life than death."
James Byrnes

Today I am aware of opportunities I did not recognize when I was drinking. Drinking stopped me from seeing the life before me. I drank myself away from the daily miracle.

In the business world, I did not see the opportunity for profit and expansion; I did not create or have faith in my ideas, and I was not able to understand or absorb new information to be successful in my life. Alcoholism kept me on the outside of my life existence.

Today I am alive in my life, creating, expanding, and enjoying my leisure. With sobriety, I have the opportunity to experience God in the many aspects of life.

Teach me to find You in the risks of life.

Honesty

"Honesty is the first chapter of the book of wisdom."
Thomas Jefferson

It is impossible to have a spiritual program without being honest. It is impossible to be recovering from addiction without being honest. A crucial aspect of sobriety is honesty.

When I was using, I was dishonest. I stopped other people from getting to know me. Part of my loneliness and isolation was caused by my dishonesty. The unmanageability that nearly destroyed my life grew in dishonesty.

Today I need to be honest—rigorously honest—even in the small things. I can no longer exist to please others; I need to please myself. I need to love myself by being honest.

God of wisdom, let me find truth in the honesty of my own life.

Faith

"The ablest persons in all walks of modern life are persons of faith."
Bruce Barton

It is important for those of us who have been crushed by the disease of addiction to have faith that life will get better. I stopped using and being codependent because the behavior was destroying me. My life was disintegrating in negative behavior and attitudes. Now I have chosen a different way to live.

Today I seek to find God in my freedom of choice, my ability to change. I have faith that my life will get better so long as I avoid those things that hurt me. My faith enables me to change.

God, may my faith in myself
reflect my belief in You.

Sex

"Sexual pleasure, wisely used and not abused, may prove the stimulus and liberator of our finest and most exalted activities."
Havelock Ellis

Sex is beautiful because it enables me, as a human being, to share love at a personal and intimate level. It joins the spiritual senses of my body, mind, and emotions in one expression, balancing tenderness with strength, patience with desire, and need with selflessness.

My awareness and experience of a beautiful sexuality should be taken into all other manifestations of life—work, leisure, friendship, and prayer, to name a few. Sex is one of my finest and most creative attributes and should not be used irresponsibly. Today I understand I have a responsibility to the gifts God has shared with me.

May I find an awareness of You in my sexuality.

Wisdom

"Education today, more than ever before, must see clearly the dual objectives: education for living and education for making a living."
James Mason Wood

The spiritual life is productive. Not only does it make for a prosperous existence, it makes for a creative lifestyle. Nothing is wasted on spiritual people; they learn from their mistakes and doubts.

For too long, I was stunted in my spiritual growth by negative and destructive thinking. I was sick and attracted equally sick people. I wanted to change. But how? As with everything else in life, I needed to imitate those who were successful. I needed to be shown how to live a different way. I needed to discover the power of my spirituality. I found successful people. They helped me. Today I am able to help myself.

Give me wisdom to imitate those
who are successful in life.

Success

"Success is a journey, not a destination."
Ben Sweetland

As long as I am sober, I know I am successful. I also know my sobriety is more than keeping away from the first drink. My sobriety requires that I be a creative and successful human being in all areas of my life: relationships, work, family, business, and acts of charity. The road to success is exactly that—a road I am traveling along. I will continue on this until the day I die. The danger is in thinking I have already arrived. As such, I get complacent and apathetic; I slow down, and energy for recovery is diminished.

Today I know I am successful as long as I keep moving with my spiritual program.

Let me always be confident
as I walk in my journey of life.

Potential

"Treat people as if they were what they ought to be, and you help them to become what they are capable of being."
Johann Wolfgang von Goethe

My program of recovery from alcoholism helps me have a relationship with myself. It helps me relate to and understand others. The more I understand my strengths and weaknesses, the more I am able to understand others.

Any understanding of spirituality involves other people. If spirituality helps me become what God intends, this is also true for others. Today I choose to treat myself and other people as children of God, remembering we were created to reach for the stars!

Loving Spirit, my potential forever rests in You.

War

"We have the power to make this the best genera-
tion of humankind in the history of the world—or
to make it the last."
John F. Kennedy

War is tragic because it always destroys. War kills creation itself. The immensity of war is such that it cannot be fully comprehended. Only isolated aspects can be understood: a child is maimed, a treaty is broken, a race is blamed, bullets are heard, and a history is ended in silence.

My addiction was a kind of war—a silent war that existed within me as an individual, and in my family. My creativity was attacked from the inside. God was forgotten in my acts of destructive selfishness.

Today I practice sobriety. My adherence to a program of recovery allows me to live in peace, one day at a time.

Teach me to make peace in my life.

February

Religion

"We have just enough religion to make us hate,
but not enough to make us love one another."
Jonathan Swift

Religion is a powerful influence in the world, but often the power is negative. It has been used to judge, divide, separate, and control people; rob them of their freedom and creativity; and chain them to creeds and teachings that are not comprehensible. Unfortunately, religion has become dull and lifeless for many people, and God's love is missed.

But the power of creative spirituality is always alive in God's world. It unites and frees people so they can be discovered in their individuality. Difference is accepted, choice is respected, and healing is perceived in our ability to love.

May I bring Your gift of spirituality
to those who have misplaced it.

Work

"We work to become, not to acquire."
Elbert Hubbard

I believe it is easier to get well than it is to stay sick, but we must be prepared to work for our sobriety. We need to confront the disease and discover the person God created in us. The road to recovery is rewarding because, as we travel it, we cast aside those aspects of our character that have been destroying us and discover our strengths, virtues, and God-given spirituality.

For years, I worked for money or security. Today I am working on myself for myself. I work at discovering God in God's world. I am finding God in my life. I realize my creative work coincides with God's will for the world.

Thank You for the gift of work
that enables me to discover more of myself.

Statistics

"There are three kinds of lies: lies, damned lies, and statistics."
Benjamin Disraeli

I used to hide behind anything—even statistics. This expanded my ego and kept me sick. Numbers confused issues by making everything complicated. In the field of alcoholism, statistics are important for comparison and research, but they are no substitute for rigorous honesty based on personal experience.

Statistics alone cannot stop a person from drinking, but sharing about personal suffering and victory produces identification that can lead to change. As a recovering alcoholic, I need to know the statistics concerning my disease, but I also need to know today's recovery is based upon yesterday's honest sharing.

Let me always see the faces behind the numbers.

Intelligence

"The brighter you are, the more you have to learn."
Don Herold

The one thing I have learned in sobriety is how much I do not know! I thought I knew a lot about God, only to discover that I had made God a prisoner of the Church. Once I was willing to free God from my prison, I discovered a freedom and an awareness that constantly fascinate and astound me.

Today I see that the glory of God shines within my pain, within my loneliness and confusion. The acceptance of my disease is the key to my recovery. Today any suffering enables me to discover a realistic spirituality—and it is okay to be confused!

With each new day, let me learn something, even if it is that I have not learned anything that day!

Money

"Capital, as such, is not evil; it is its wrong use that is evil."
Mohandas K. Gandhi

I am not afraid to say I am concerned for my prosperity —not just in terms of health, friendship, and employment but also in terms of money. For years, I wanted to have the best and not shortchange myself, and I felt guilty. In sobriety, I know I deserve the best. Money, prosperity, and capital are not bad in themselves; it is how I use them that matters.

Today, as promised in recovery, things are getting better, and I am able to invest and buy wisely. I am able to appreciate and share my monetary benefits. Family, friends, and the needy can genuinely share my prosperity: The more I give away today, the more I get.

May I always use the gift of money responsibly.

Lies

"Convictions are more dangerous enemies of truth than lies."
Frederick Nietzche

I know if a lie is spoken loudly enough, often enough, and with enough ceremony and ritual, people will believe it. I identify with this statement: "I said I was not alcoholic because I did not drink every day, or in the mornings, or all day. Besides, I was too young!"

As a practicing alcoholic, people believed me when I lied. Many people still believe this lie about themselves. Spirituality requires that I not only confront the lies in other people but also those in myself.

Usually, if I am angry at the remarks of others, it is because they remind me of myself. Today I seek not to condemn but to understand.

May I continue to learn about myself
from the criticism I direct at others.

Childlike

"In every child who is born, under no matter what circumstances, and of no matter what parents, the potentiality of the human race is born again."
James Agee

Today I see and believe the God-given dignity of the human race in the faces and lifestyles of others. In the challenge and rebelliousness of youth, there is the hope for tomorrow. I associate myself with the need to question, risk, and be outrageous. I play and laugh at myself and own my craziness. I do not need to be perfect. When I used drugs, I was judgmental, serious, and controlling. Everything had to have a place, an answer, or be acceptable to others. My guilt was caused by my inability to please others.

Today I can be childlike and identify with the radical message for tomorrow: "To thine own self be true!"

*God, I see a child looking at the stars
and I smile. I am that child.*

Hope

"The hopeful person sees success where others see failure, sunshine where others see shadows and storm."

O. S. Marden

Spirituality involves my attitudes and perceptions, as well as my prayers. It requires awareness of what I need and what I have been given. Spirituality sees beyond any problem into the solution.

Hope is a feeling based on a spiritual perception of life that shuns apathy and negativity. Everything can be used for good if it is perceived realistically. I can use destructive experiences, painful moments, and failed relationships to create a new tomorrow. The hope that stems from my ability to change requires understanding what has happened. Because it points to my glorious tomorrows, no aspect of my life should be wasted.

Teach me the secret of success
in the problems of life.

Environment

"Love your neighbor as yourself, but choose your neighbor."
Louise Beal

Part of my recovery and sobriety involves change. It is not enough to put down the jug to gain sobriety; I need to make substantial changes in my life.

Where I live, with whom I live, the friends I keep, and the relationships I make are crucial to my sobriety. Human beings imitate. They imitate clothes, hairstyles, and mannerisms. Sobriety is also imitated.

As a recovering alcoholic, I can only be spiritually happy with those who are joyous and free. I need to find them.

God, You are to be found in all creation.
Let me seek you in a noble lifestyle.

Insight

"Nothing is more terrible than activity without insight."
Thomas Carlyle

I believe recovery can only begin when we see or start to get a glimpse of who we are and what we are dealing with. Insight begins with insight into self. However, the moment we begin to "see" must be followed by a determined effort to discover more—digging through the denial, pain, and manipulation to the disease.

After discovering the disease in our lives, we must be prepared to risk talking about it on a daily basis.

Recovery requires a daily desire to see, discover, and talk about our addiction. With this insight comes recovery.

You are the light of the world.
Shine through my honesty.

Pity

*"When a person has pity on all living creatures,
only then is one noble."*
Buddhist Saying

We all need each other. More than this, we need to help and sustain each other. This concept extends beyond human beings, for the world is full of other creatures God has made that make our lives fascinating and entertaining. Animals and plants constitute our ecological history, yet we often rob and hurt our environment.

Recovery from alcoholism means more than putting down the drink. Today I adopt a responsible attitude that makes me care, on a spiritual level, for my world.

*God, as I look around my world,
I cannot help but honor You.*

Freedom

"Freedom comes from human beings, rather than from laws and institutions."
Clarence Darrow

The disease of alcoholism does not live in bottles or books; it lives in people. Drug problems are people problems. It follows that sobriety exists in the person, not the theory.

In this sense, recovery must be experienced, rather than simply pondered or discussed. The essence of the Program is not written in books or taught in lecture rooms but lived in the lives of people; the Program stems from the heart.

I believe the Program is that spark of Divinity that God has bestowed upon all of us, and we must discover it within.

Teach me that to think a smile
without revealing it is to be grumpy.

Reality

*"It is the chiefest point of happiness that
humankind is willing to be what it is."*
Desiderius Erasmus

I am an alcoholic. Today I am able to love myself
because I am able to accept myself.

Because I am able to accept myself, I am able to be
myself. The acceptance of my disease of alcoholism has
taught me that I am not perfect and I do not live in a
perfect world. This leads to an acceptance of others. My
pain around alcohol has given me an insight into the sufferings of others, and this has produced spiritual growth
in me. I am happy not because I am an alcoholic but
because I know that I am an alcoholic. Today I can be
what I was meant to be, rather than the fake I was
becoming.

In the spiritual journey to You is my happiness.

Love

"Let there be spaces in your togetherness."
Kahlil Gibran

As an alcoholic, I demanded love and was possessive of others. I selfishly treated people as possessions and made them responsible for my own satisfaction and survival. My fear of being alone caused me to blackmail people with my needs and emotions.

Today I love people while allowing them to breathe. My program entails healthy detachment. I take responsibility for me and allow others to take responsibility for themselves. I give those I love the space they need. Sometimes, I must love people enough to let them go. I am beginning to understand that to be free, I must give freedom to others.

God, in the spaces of my love
is the growth experienced.

Humility

"What makes humility so desirable is the marvelous thing it does to us; it creates in us a capacity for the closest possible intimacy with God."
Monica Baldwin

Humility is not so much about trying to be good as accepting that I am imperfect. For too long, I thought humility was keeping the peace, appearing to be perfect, bottling up my anger and resentments, living a life of people-pleasing.

Today I understand that humility is being real. It is accepting my humanity and being honest in my relationships. Humility is respecting the lives of others while respecting my own. Humility is seeking to reveal the Divinity that God has given to my life. Humility is knowing that in the lives of my fellow human beings, the good and the bad are reflected in me.

God, let me have the humility to be real.

Enemies

"The Bible tells us to love our neighbors and also to love our enemies, probably because they are generally the same people."
G. K. Chesterton

My spiritual program makes me look to where I am, rather than where I want to be. I live in the now, rather than the never-never land of tomorrow.

To love my world, I seek to understand the people who live in it. This entails acceptance of those who are different from me. I must build bridges rather than barriers. It is easy for me to talk about loving and being concerned for the starving millions while forgetting to love and relate to my coworker or neighbor.

I have experience with people who are difficult because I lived with my addicted self for many years. I am the key to my enemies.

Teach me to accept in love those,
for today, I do not like.

Belonging

"But one day . . . it came to me that feeling of being part of everything, not separate at all. I knew that if I cut a tree, my arm would bleed."
Alice Walker

I am aware of the truth that I belong. I am an essential part of God's world. I share Divinity because God made me. Today I seek the spiritual center in me that is forever positive and creative. I am the center of my universe.

Past hurts and wrongs cannot take away the uniqueness in my life. Past abuses and painful put-downs, my years of alternating between the lost child or the scapegoat in my family, need not make me a victim. I am free to choose recovery and acceptance of self. I associate with the winners of this world. I participate in Creation by being a creative person for me. Yesterday's pain has no power in my life today.

When I kneel before the stream, mountains, and stars, I feel You, God.

Law

"The life of the law has not been logic; it has been experience."
Oliver Wendell Holmes, Jr

I respect the law. I respect the society in which I live. I am not an island unto myself. I live in a community and have a responsibility to myself and others; such is sobriety.

For years, I did what I wanted and tried not to be found out. I was manipulative, dishonest, and unhappy. Then I decided to change my life. I discovered the spiritual law of freedom through responsibility. Law is the collective experience of the many who choose to live a certain way, and today I choose to live among them. My understanding of spirituality involves respecting the laws that give me the dignity of citizenship.

Dear God, help me see that the laws of civilization are a gift of freedom.

Prejudice

"The chief cause of human error is to be found in the prejudices picked up in childhood."
René Descartes

I have begun to recognize how many of my prejudices were planted in childhood. Family, teachers, clergy, and friends passed prejudices on to me: "The Jews are bad because they killed Jesus." "Whites are superior to others." "Women should obey the man of the house." "Gays are child molesters." "Sex is for having babies, and you should not enjoy it."

Today I live with the problem of knowing these statements are untrue, but a part of me is still affected by them. My spiritual program demands that I expose prejudice for the hate it is and that I try to pass on to the next generation the joy that comes from love, acceptance, and freedom.

Let Your children, including me,
grow in freedom.

Christianity

"Going to Church doesn't make you a Christian
any more than going to the garage makes you a
car."
Laurence J. Peter

I believe Christianity is about bringing humankind
together, rather than creating division and resentment.
It must be much bigger than what we do or say in any
building. Christ's truth seeks to discover God in the
splendor of this varied world.

My addiction made me a small person with a small
god. Constantly focusing on differences in the world
stopped me from seeing the glaring similarities. The
world of black and white, rather than shades of creative
color, is sick and dangerous. Christ reveals for me the
bridge by which reconciliation and harmony are
achieved. The message is not so much dogma as a
revealed journey into Truth.

In the created stranger,
help me discover the friend.

Art

"Only work which is the product of inner compulsion can have spiritual meaning."
Walter Gropius

I have developed, in my recovery, an awareness of the beauty of this world and an appreciation of what people can produce. Sobriety has made art accessible. Today I see beauty in paintings, sculpture, music, literature, and the art of nature.

Spirituality is always creative; it is at the center of all that is good, noble, and inspiring. Although I may not be an artist, I appreciate and have a feeling of belonging to the beauty of this world. In a sense, it all happens and takes shape through me. The rediscovery of spirituality has brought the world and the universe into my life.

Give me the desire to re-create
Your splendor through my experiences.

Patriotism

"For us, patriotism is the same as the love of humanity."
Mohandas K. Gandhi

I am on the side of humankind. I am convinced my welfare is generated by the peace and stability of the world. The love that produces spiritual growth stems from my relationships in the world; we cannot exist alone.

Today I strive to bring the world and people together. We must seek not to be the same but rather to rejoice in the richness of difference. Drugs always divide, separate, and isolate; spirituality unites. I am an optimist for humankind because of what has happened in my own life.

Thank You for a humanity that can be shared.

Thought

"I was a free thinker before I knew how to think."
George Bernard Shaw

Everyone is influenced by someone, and so am I. To not be influenced is to remain ignorant. Today I do not hinder my thinking, particularly around spiritual matters, because of pride. I may not like change. I may find it hard to accept attitudes and opinions that differ from my own. I know pride keeps me deaf and often stupid. However, the daily program of a lived spirituality encourages a variety of opinions and attitudes. I can learn from different customs, lifestyles, and religions. I can be helped in my understanding of life by the stranger.

I know I do not have all the answers. Today I am prepared to listen.

Sustainer of all religions and philosophies,
help me discover You in any differences.

Self

*"The Spirit of God hath made me, and the breath
of the Almighty hath given me life."*
Job 33:4

My spiritual journey involves a discovery of self. For years, I pretended to be what I was not, what I imagined myself to be, or what others wanted me to be.

Today I am beginning to know myself. I understand my needs and my strengths. I accept my weaknesses and live with my confusion. From the time I put down the glass, things have progressively gotten better, but there is still a great deal I do not understand. The daily violence and suffering, and my own personal greed, cowardice, and arrogance—where do they come from? I do not know, and that is okay. I still search. My suspicion is that the answer lies within my own insecurities.

*In Your time, God, may I grow
in my understanding of self.*

Ambition

"The child without ambition is like a watch with a broken spring."
R. W. Stockman

It is not wrong to have ambition. It is not wrong to want to be somebody. The tragedy is that this has to be said!

For too long, I played the tapes in my head that discouraged ambition and creative pride. I confused humility with timidity and self-abuse. I waited for things to happen, rather than making them happen for myself.

Today I know I am a creature of God, created to create. God is at work in my life. I am part of God's miracle for the world.

God, may I always have ambition for those things that are good and true.

Uniqueness

"Each honest calling, each walk of life, has its own elite, its own aristocracy, based upon excellence of performance."
James Bryant Conant

In the past, I was so busy admiring the gifts of others that I missed my own; I was so caught up in the lives of others that I missed my own existence. One of the symptoms of my alcoholism was low self-esteem. Of course, I acted in a role of confidence. I pretended everything was okay. I wore the mask of success, but deep within I was always waiting for the world to find out I was a fake, that something was missing in my life.

In recovery, I have discovered God's gift of spirituality. I know through my life that a uniqueness exists in the world. I have the capacity to make the day better, not only for myself but also for others.

Thank You for the specialness of my life.

Facts

"To treat your facts with imagination is one thing, but to imagine your facts is another."
John Burroughs

When I was drinking, I always confused fantasy with reality. Lies got mingled with facts, and facts became exaggerated. It was almost impossible for me to distinguish between reality and fantasy, imagination and fact. My life was a complicated lie.

Today I have a program of rigorous honesty. I must be rigorous and stop the game before it starts. I practice the principles of recovery in every area of my life. The spiritual road involves a comprehensive journey, and nothing need be left out.

God, who created the mountains, help me take responsibility for the grit between my toes.

Perfection

"God, the Good, is the basic power you express."
Robert Bitzer

It is so easy for me to focus on the failings of others and miss my own. My attraction to gossip allows me to criticize other people while keeping the attention away from me. Sometimes I feel good by exposing the weaknesses of others.

This attitude needs to be changed if I am to fully enjoy the fruits of sobriety. I do not need to be drinking to behave like a drunk; gossip and character assassination are reminiscent of my past addictive behavior. I do not need the side of me that seeks to destroy the character of others. With my spiritual program, I am seeking to change.

May I grow in forgiveness
and acceptance of others.

Change

"Nothing stays the same. When you think you've got something down, it changes!"
Leo Booth

I am aware life is about change. Even the familiar trans-forms at some point. When I was drinking, I hated change. I wanted to control everything and everyone; things had to be my way. Naturally, when accused of needing to be in charge, I replied, "Certainly not!" The addict's disease is fed by illusion and denial.

Today I take a leap of faith and trust the universe will still be around in the morning and will probably look much the same. I seek to accept, one day at a time, that variety really is the spice of life and must include the awkward ingredient of change.

Creator, I accept and welcome the
spiritual ingredient of change in my life.

Understanding

"Understanding is the reward of faith. Therefore, seek not to understand that thou mayest believe, but believe that thou mayest understand."
Saint Augustine

I understand that God is love. It makes more sense to live my life with love than with anger, resentment, or despair. I know the answer to life, with any problems that may arise, is love: not simply loving those people who love me, but beginning to love and understand those who dislike or hate me. Being imperfect people in an imperfect world produces enemies.

Today I love my world by listening to my critics, changing unreasonable attitudes, and growing in the humility that comes from silence. Change is part of God's blessing of love. This I believe. This I understand. And, step by step, it is beginning to work in my life.

May my love for the world give me
an understanding of self.

Integrity

"Persons of integrity, by their very existence, rekindle the belief that as a people we can live above the level of moral squalor."
John Gardner

I understand integrity to be a willingness to make sacrifices for what we believe to be true. Living a spiritual program must lead to integrity.

Not so many years ago, integrity was not a word in my vocabulary because of my unwillingness to make sacrifices. I was so selfishly preoccupied with my wants that I gave little thought to the needs of others. The more I lost myself in self, the greater was the emotional pain.

Today I live the paradox that only in giving do I truly receive.

May I express the paradox of sacrifice in my life.

Genius

*"The principal mark of genius is not perfection
but originality, the opening of new frontiers."*
Arthur Koestler

I need to remember that genius is often simplicity itself.
The original thought need not be abstract, intellectual,
or technical; thoughts exist to transmit the message.

In the slogans "Keep It Simple," "One Day at a
Time," and "Don't Pick Up the First Drink," wisdom
combines with simplicity to produce sobriety. God is at
work everywhere and the spiritual message always brings
healing. AA is more than a "fellowship of genius"; it is
Divinity set to a program. What began with a group of
alcoholics crosses new frontiers into the healing of the
world.

*God of Truth, may I always be open
and receptive to Your voice.*

Hell

"The hottest places in Hell are reserved for those who, in time of great moral crises, maintain their neutrality."
Dante Alighieri

Often, we create a personal hell not by what we perpetrate but by what we allow to happen. Much of the loneliness and isolation addicts and their families experience results from remaining hidden and silent. The pretense that everything is okay is not only untrue but deadly.

Today I choose not to be neutral. I speak about my alcoholism to wage war against the disease that nearly killed me. I speak out about addiction so society cannot say it did not know what was happening. I speak up for treatment and recovery because I know they work in the vast majority of cases. I am not neutral when it comes to addiction because I am fighting for my life.

Give me the courage to speak up in a crowd. Let me live the message I was privileged to receive.

Identity

"Without freedom, no one really has a name."
Milton Acorda

Part of my identity involves my disease. I am an alcoholic and my name is. . . . With this recognition of who I am come the liberty and freedom to live and create in God's world. Who I am involves what I am; in the fusion of the two is my spiritual identity.

For years, I ran from myself because I wanted to be different. I felt I would not be acceptable or good enough for you. In running from me, I lost my identity; the seed of low self-esteem was sown.

Knowing I can only be who I am brings the freedom of existence and identity. I am what I am!

Lord, You once said, "I am that I am."
Well, so am I!

Hypocrisy

"Hypocrisy: prejudice with a halo."
Ambrose Bierce

As a religious person, I could be a hypocrite. I thought my goodness depended on judging others as inferior. I put others down so I could appear terrific. Part of me knew I was wrong. I ignored religious teachings that emphasize forgiveness and acceptance and instead focused on judgment and condemnation. It was all part of my sickness. Inside, I was hurting and feeling guilty, but I hid behind a mask of respectability.

Today I accept the nonreligious and rejoice in different cultures and creeds. I do not fear those who are different, and I am slowly beginning to accept my own imperfections.

You who have loved me through forgiveness,
help me to forgive.

Ideals

"An idealist is one who, on noticing a rose smells better than a cabbage, concludes it will also make better soup."
H. L. Mencken

My spiritual program teaches me to be an idealist with my feet on the ground. People will continue to hurt, get angry, and tell lies; wrestling with imperfections is not just my problem. I accept that I live in an imperfect world and recovery involves reality, not illusion.

My responsibility in recovery is for my life. I cannot change other people, events, or relationships; I can only change me. I am not God. Each time I forget this fact, I risk another hurt.

Help me aspire to ideals within my grasp.

Doubt

"Sixty years ago, I knew everything; now I know nothing. Education is a progressive discovery of our own ignorance."
Will Durant

Spirituality is knowing I do not know. It is waking up in the morning with my eyes fully open, awaiting the adventure of the new day. New things, theories, and facts are discovered every day, and this makes for a glorious and exciting world.

There was a time when I used knowledge to protect myself from the challenges and inconsistencies of life. God had to be a proven fact, evidenced in theory and dogma. As such, the mystery was lost.

Today my relationship with God is real. Doubt has become part of my faith. The state of not knowing is creative and stimulating. To not know is the beginning of wisdom.

You who have spoken through wind and fire, speak through my doubts.

Greed

"Not one who has little, but one who wishes more, is poor."
Seneca

In recovery, I still must deal with the compulsive side of my nature that always wants more. I must remember to be grateful for what I have. I try not to hold up a code of behavior I expect from others but not myself! I know I miss the fun of the moment when I am preoccupied with what I may be missing elsewhere. I know I miss the comfort of my own home as I fantasize about country mansions. Always I want more, yet in my own experience more has always been less.

Today I focus on a spiritual program of gratitude. I have a checklist of things to be grateful for. I work on my greed by talking about it.

*Thank You for the part of me
that must remain poor.*

Science

"We have to live today by what truth we can get today and be ready tomorrow to call it falsehood."
William James

To change is to be imperfect, and to be imperfect is to be wrong at times! As an alcoholic, I have a problem with ego, always wanting to be right, hating to say "I am sorry," and not wishing to appear out of control. In sobriety, I must wrestle with my ego on a daily basis.

Although I find it difficult to accept that I am imperfect, I know I am! I know I need to make amends. I know I produce most of the pain in my life. Today's facts are stepping stones to tomorrow's falsehoods, and I grow with this knowledge. Spirituality is growing in the knowledge that I do not have all the answers.

Let me experience joy and growth in the dilemmas of life.

Profit

*"In freeing people . . . our country's blessing will
also come, for profit follows righteousness."*
Senator Albert Beveridge

Profit is more than financial benefit or material well-
being. For the recovering alcoholic or drug addict, it
is being aware of life, feeling feelings, and having the
capacity for a relationship with God, self, and others. But
financial benefit is also part of spirituality. The blessing
of money and economic stability is part of God's love
and trust. This gift of freedom involves responsibility
and stewardship.

With money and profit, not only am I able to enjoy
creative comforts, but I can also help make the lives of
others creative. A responsible use of money is part of my
recovery program and has become one of the joys of my
spiritual awakening.

*Let Your blessing of money in life
help me to bless others.*

Dreams

"If one advances confidently in the direction of one's dreams and endeavors to live the life which one has imagined, one will meet with a success unexpected in common hours."
Henry David Thoreau

Drugs brought me nightmares, never dreams. For years, I lived in fear. In the night, I imagined horrible shapes, strange colors and sounds, experienced unspeakable tortures, and awoke in tension and sweat.

Today in sobriety, my dreams are serene and tranquil. I remember friends, loved ones, and those I most admire. I imagine God in the beauty of Creation.

God breathes love through me. My dreams are part of my wellness.

God, who created people to dream
their dreams, help me live mine.

Balance

"There are two ways to slide easily through life:
to believe everything or to doubt everything.
Both ways save us from thinking."
Alfred Korzybski

In the past, I was not only compulsive and obsessive about things I believed in but also about things I did not believe in. I was extreme. All I did was exaggerated. I either raced through life at warp speed or I was in neutral. Balance was absent.

Today I am developing balance in my life through patience and tolerance. My extremism was a mask behind which I hid from life. I did not have to think, consider, or ponder; I simply reacted.

I know that to believe in everything is to believe in nothing, and to doubt everything is to not think. Life is a many-splendored thing, and it has a variety of options.

God of the many, help me discover You
in the myriad thoughts life produces.

Wine

"Wine that maketh glad the heart of humankind."
Psalm 104:15

Every good thing can be abused, and alcohol is no exception. Although most people are able to enjoy the fruits of the grape and the quality of their lives is enriched by good wine, not a few are destroyed by it!

Millions of people in the world are alcoholics—myself included. I did not want to be alcoholic, but I am. My life and relationships were slowly being destroyed by alcohol. I had to stop drinking to find happiness.

God can be appreciated in the grape and can just as easily be experienced in a soda. I must find healthy new ways to be happy.

Thank You for the precious gift of choice.

Thought

"By thought I embrace the universal."
Blaise Pascal

My ability to think and communicate allows me not only to live in this world but also to understand it. When I do not think, I am usually irresponsible.

Alcohol stopped me from thinking and behaving responsibly and created dishonesty in my life. Instead of feeling I belonged, I felt I was on the outside. Instead of enjoying relationships, I was forever involved in bitter disputes. Instead of enjoying the peace of being a child of God, I felt like an abandoned creature. My problem was alcohol, and I had to do something about it. I did. I stopped taking the first drink. Today I am alive in God's world and enjoying this universe.

When I think clearly, I know I belong.

Risk

"A free society is one where it is safe to be unpopular."
Adlai Stevenson

At times, tough love requires me to say or do things that make me unpopular. That is part of the spiritual risk of loving. As an alcoholic, I was a people-pleaser, concerned with saying and doing what people wanted and remaining silent rather than causing upset. I was afraid if I said what I really thought, I might be rejected. My self-esteem was secondary to what other people thought of me.

In sobriety, I love myself enough to say what I believe and do what I consider right. I refuse to remain silent when confronted with injustice or the addictions of others. My spiritual program risks the possibility of being unpopular.

Teach me to always say and do
what I believe is true.

Saints

"Saints are the sinners who keep on going."
Robert Louis Stevenson

At times, I do not want to carry on; I do not want to fight anymore for truth and freedom. At times, it seems so much easier to give up and agree with everybody, but deep inside I know this is not true.

Occasionally, the disease speaks to me and tells me to give up and everything will be okay: "Maybe you can have one drink." "Don't rush off to so many meetings." "Get what you can when you can!" It all sounds so tempting, but I know it does not work.

Sobriety works! The struggle and pain to act responsibly in my life are paying off, and it does get better. I am not going to give up. My life is worth more than a quick fix!

*Spirit, let me know true courage
is working through the pain.*

Humor

"Humor may be defined as the kindly contempla-
tion of the incongruities of life and the artistic
impression thereof. . . . The essence of humor is
human kindliness."
Stephen Leacock

Humor for me is a key to balance. In a joke, I am able
to release a little tension or frustration and cope
with my disease of alcoholism. When I drank, I did not
have a genuine sense of humor; it was sarcasm, cruel put-
downs, and insane expressions of my manic personality.
My fun was created at the expense of others. It was a
form of violence. It kept people away from me and created loneliness in my life.

Today I use humor as an expression of acceptance, tolerance, understanding, and forgiveness. Humor is an
aspect of my spiritual program. In humor, I experience
God.

Give me the gift of humor that
reflects dignity and hope for us all.

Madness

"Sanity is madness put to good use."
George Santayana

The phrase "Make the disease work for you" makes a great deal of sense. I am a recovering alcoholic. My alcoholism is still with me, so every day I take the necessary steps to stay sober.

My disease is the "mad" part of me that wants to destroy my life, relationships, and understanding of God. I need to accept my "madness" and turn it around so that it works for me. My suffering is a key to my spiritual growth. My anger helps me understand the imperfections of others. My powerlessness over alcohol gives me an understanding of humility based in reality. The acceptance of my "madness" keeps me sane!

Loving Spirit, give me the sanity to accept my imperfections and grow into the best I can be.

Apathy

"Science may have found a cure for most evils,
but it has found no remedy for the worst of them
all—the apathy of human beings."
Helen Keller

I read of a man who overate until he died. When interviewed, friends and family said, "He simply didn't seem to care." He had stuffed his feelings for so long he had forgotten what they were. He had lost his spirituality. Apathy can kill.

Apathy feeds ignorance because it stops activity; it stops life. My antidote for apathy is spirituality. Spiritual people are alive with positive attitudes and creative hope, and they are infectious. I am challenged to discover meaning in my own life. Hope supports recovery, and recovery produces a message that must be shared. In that message is the miracle of life.

I pray that in the face of apathy I discover hope.

Humanity

"I love my country better than my family; but I love humanity better than my country."
François Fenélon

I need to think big. I must escape from the little concepts that keep me small. Life is more than I can ever perceive. I need to see it in its totality.

The nuclear family can be restrictive if viewed as the center of loyalty. Even national citizenship should be placed in the context of the world. My freedom rests in universal humanity.

Spirituality is about thinking big. It is finding God in the richness of creation. Shared humanity is the path to world peace and serenity. Divisions should not exist for the humanitarian who seeks acceptance for all individuals simply because they are people.

*God, may I seek and find the One
in the many and the many in the One.*

Forgiveness

"God will forgive me; that's God's business."
Heinrich Heine

It took me a long time to accept that God had forgiven the deeds of my addiction. It took me a long time to comprehend that God is forgiveness, forgiving love. Forgiveness unites us with God because it is God's nature to forgive.

When I am living the spiritual life, I unite myself with God by my acts of forgiveness. When I forgive others, I am perfecting a kindness, an act of forgiveness, to myself.

Hate used to drain me of energy, and it still can if I get caught up in resentments. Forgiveness restores energy and peace. When I forgive, I am one with God.

*Through my forgiveness of others,
may I discover myself.*

Self-Love

"No matter how old you get, if you keep the desire to be creative, you're keeping the woman/man-child alive."
John Cassavetes

As a child, I played in the sand and made castles. I would build a fortress wall around the castle so it could withstand the wash of the waves. Today I build behavioral structures that withstand pressure and stress. I need to build my life on a sure foundation—and that foundation must be me! I take care of me so that I can enjoy my life.

How do I take care of me? As a recovering alcoholic, I choose not to drink alcohol. This is an important part of my self-love. I exercise regularly and watch what I eat. I rest in the evenings and take walks in the fresh air. The child that is in me still lives, but today that child is healthy.

*Help me treat life responsibly
but not too seriously.*

Language

"Language is the light of the mind."
John Stuart Mill

When I was drinking, I never really thought about how I behaved, how I dressed, or the language I used. Today I am responsible for the whole of me.

Language is important because it is my bridge to others. It is also a vehicle for understanding the ideas of others. Spirituality involves the concept of language because it is a means of growth, communication, and relationship. My words help me be known. My ability to understand the ideas and aspirations of others helps me feel I belong.

God is perceived in this world, and the gift of language is one of the ways God is revealed. My words are spiritual.

May the light of Your eternal truth manifest in the way I relate to others through words.

Perseverance

"I know of no more encouraging fact than the unquestionable ability of humans to elevate their lives by a conscious endeavor."
Henry David Thoreau

Life is exciting to me when I am creating, when I am pursuing a dream, and when I am making miracles in my life.

I suppose perseverance stems from a belief that things get better when we roll up our sleeves and do something. Sobriety is about comprehending that in our lives we reflect the message.

God has created humanity with the ability to make the dream come true. This is not to say it is easy, but it is harder not to dream!

Teach me to wonder at the stars
with a spade in my hands.

Teaching

"The art of teaching is the art of assisting discovery."
Mark Van Doren

I need a "sponsor" in recovery. A sponsor is someone I turn to when I have problems, when I am confused or in pain, when I need to talk, when I feel lonely, or when I am about to make a major change. I greatly benefit from someone with whom to share ideas, especially ideas that affect my actual living, because the disease of alcoholism pervades my life!

My sponsor guides, suggests, and gently leads me in the right direction. He or she does not demand, dictate, or try to be a fixer. My sponsor is a friend I can trust. My sponsor does not allow me to escape into his or her life or become addicted to our relationship.

God, let me always be free enough
to discover You in my life.

Guilt

"It is all the same to me whether one comes from Sing Sing or Harvard. We hire a person, not their history."

Henry Ford

Too often I get so locked into my history—what I did, what I said, and the events of which I was ashamed—that I miss the gift of the new day. Those who suffer from the disease of addiction need to deal with past problems but not live in them.

My attitude toward today need not be based on what happened yesterday. Today is the beginning of the rest of my life.

I know I create most of the pain and tragedy in my life, but I also know I create the joys and successes. I am confident my sobriety makes me a winner.

Spirit, I forgive myself for yesterday and look forward to the healing that comes today.

Future

"The future is hidden even from those who made it."

Anatole France

Life is a glorious mystery. I will never fully understand it. It will always confuse and amaze me. After I have understood one thing, I am presented with a fresh problem. I am not perfect. I am not God.

Years ago, this angered and irritated me. I wanted to know everything. I wanted to have the answer to all life's problems. I wanted the power that comes with perfection. I hated being vulnerable, weak, and confused! I hated being human. Yes, that was my problem. I hated being a human being.

Today I enjoy the adventure of life. I kneel in awe at life's mingled complexity. Now life is a paradox I can live with.

Help me accept the mystery of life.

Opinions

"Opinions cannot survive if one has no chance to fight for them."
Thomas Mann

As a result of my sobriety, I have opinions on a great number of subjects. Drugs have a tendency to make insane remarks appear brilliant. Drunks often see themselves as unsung poets or victimized geniuses when they are "in alcohol." I did not have opinions when I was drinking but rather a series of chaotic and incoherent reactions.

Today I have considered opinions. I am able to think and make decisions. I make a contribution to life and the world in which I live. I am involved. More than this, I have the spiritual confidence to fight for what I believe and speak out my concerns in love. I am alive, and I love it!

Let me always hear the opinions of others
but not fail to express my own.

Reason

"For here we are not afraid to follow wherever it may lead, or to tolerate error so long as reason is free to combat it."
Thomas Jefferson

As an alcoholic, I was often afraid to challenge the thinking and ideas of other people. My people-pleasing demanded peace at any price. Yet I did not agree with so much of what I heard, read, and practiced. Now I see that my attitude and behavior—along with my alcohol consumption—kept me sick.

In my spiritual program, I am free to reject, consider, and have my own opinions in life. I do not have to agree with everything that is said. In this way, I am discovering my value and self-esteem.

Lord, I am grateful for the freedom to cooperate.

World

"All wars are civil wars, because all persons are brothers and sisters. . . . Each one owes infinitely more to the human race than to the particular country in which one was born."
François Fenélon

The disease of addiction kept me separate, isolated, and alone. I was so busy seeing how I was different from other people that I missed the similarities. I missed the oneness of creation by always placing myself above it, below it, or outside it; and I was the loser.

Even my religion kept me separate. By being Christian, I was not a Jew, Muslim, or Hindu. As such, I failed to see the similarities of these major philosophies. I also failed to recognize what all religious people have in common: the inclusiveness of Love, Truth, and Forgiveness.

God is found in the difference and sameness of all people.

Dear God, I am discovering that differences, when understood, become similarities.

Time

"I would if I could stand on a busy corner, hat in hand, and beg people throw me their wasted hours."

Bernard Berenson

I enjoy sobriety so much that I hate to waste my time. Part of my spiritual program involves a correct use of time. I do not spend time with negative or destructive people. I do not spend time doing things I do not enjoy just to please others. I enjoy life so much that I do not wish to waste any of it.

As an alcoholic, I wasted too much time. For most of my life, I was "out to lunch!" Today I spend time enjoying life, and I spend quality time alone with "self." I like conversations with myself, the thoughts I need to ponder. I also need time to rest in the peace of my day. Time is a precious gift from God that should not be wasted.

God, let me live each day as if it were my last.

Problems

"The real problem is in the hearts and minds of humankind."
Albert Einstein

I am facing not so much a "drug problem" as a "people problem," and this requires a solution that comes from me. I believe my solution and recovery have already been given by God but must be discovered from within.

I need to seek out what is truly in my mind and heart: What are my problems, what are my needs, what do I long for, and where am I going in my life?

It is no longer enough for me to know my problems; I need also talk about them. Today I choose to express my feelings.

God, I thank You for the creative gift
of communication.

Wonder

"We love to wonder, and that is the seed of science."
Ralph Waldo Emerson

In sobriety, the world is a wonderful place. I often sit back and am amazed at the splendor of life, the simple happenings that bring such joy, the nobility that is revealed in humankind, and the creative adventure and mystery of life.

I see how drugs kept me blind to so much. Alcohol held me prisoner to mediocrity, and much of the wonder of life passed me by. As a drinking alcoholic, I existed rather than lived life. I was a bored spectator rather than a participant. I reacted to things, rather than initiating events. Alcoholism equals dullness. Recovery symbolizes energy. Today I dream dreams and bask in the wonder of it all.

Divine Spirit, let me see the wonderful
mystery of life even in the ordinary.

Beauty

"Beauty is not caused. It is."
Emily Dickinson

So many people think beauty is what we do to ourselves: makeup, clothes, hairstyles, or jewelry. It is so easy to get caught up in conditions. Reality is not about what we do but who we are.

The beauty God created comes from within: the twinkle in someone's eyes that says "Hello," the hug that says "I love you," the gentle embrace and smile that say "I forgive you," or the tear that cries "I understand."

When God said to the world, "It is good, and very good," beauty was born. Drugs, alcohol, or crazy relationships only get in the way of my being what I was intended to be—beautiful for God.

Today I seek to put Your beauty
in my actions, words, and attitudes.

Failure

"No one is a failure who is enjoying life."
William Feather

Spirituality is fun. I enjoy my sobriety today, and I do not take myself too seriously.

For years I thought I was a failure, and this thought manifested the behavior of failure. I hid, sulked, was jealous, carried resentments, and isolated myself from life, then blamed the world.

Today because I really understand and accept that I am a child of God, I know I am not a failure. I have a glorious future in recovery. I have hope. I have confidence. I am able to accept and forgive. I am able to love my neighbor because I love myself.

In my enjoyment of life, may I reflect
Your love for the world.

Pride

"Though pride is not a virtue, it is the parent of many virtues."
M. C. Collins

Pride is not necessarily negative. It is sensible to have a balanced pride in sobriety because self-esteem grows from the pride and respect I give myself.

Balanced pride helps me with my appearance, grooming, and etiquette. Pride helps me with my communication skills: I work hard at being understood, speaking out clearly, and developing better methods of being understood.

Pride stops me from being taken advantage of: It enables me to say no to others while still feeling good about myself. A healthy sense of pride is essential for spiritual growth.

Creator, let me have a realistic appreciation of myself that leads to achievement.

Aging

"You just wake up one morning and you got it!"
Moms Mabley

I am so busy living I do not think about getting old. I am so grateful in my recovery from alcoholism that tomorrow, the future, and age are secondary.

In my sickness, I was always living in the future: What will tomorrow bring? Will I die crippled, lonely, and afraid? My projections into the future produced emotional pain.

Today I do not need to do this. I welcome age because I bring into it the joy and experience of my sobriety. My spiritual program reminds me to be grateful for my life, and this includes the inevitability of aging.

Lord, as I grow in age, may I also grow
in wisdom and tolerance.

Lies

"It takes a wise person to handle a lie; a fool had better remain honest."
Norman Douglas

As a drinking alcoholic, I told so many lies to cover the lies I had previously told that I got lost in a maze of untruth! Most of the lies were stupid, irrelevant, and harmless, but they were all aimed at building up my ego. My memory could not keep up with my tongue, and I became guilty, ashamed, and embarrassed.

Today I remember there is nothing any lie can give me. There is nothing in the world of fabrication from which I might benefit. I already have everything I need. I have a relationship with God and friends I understand and with whom I can be vulnerable. I do not need to be perfect to be loved.

*Help me seek the good life
in those things that are good.*

Service

"No one is useless in this world who lightens the burdens of another."
Charles Dickens

As a drunk, I thought the world owed me a living, everyone existed for my employment and service, and the world was waiting for my telephone call. For years, I manipulated people. I was such a good con artist that they often left thanking me!

Today part of my spiritual program requires service. I make the coffee, put out the cookies, cook the meal, and invite friends for dinner. I make the telephone call, give the lectures, share in groups, and write articles. My life of service helps keep me sober. I am the message I share, and I do it for me!

*Thank You for making me aware
of my need to give.*

Today

"Real generosity toward the future consists in giving all to what is present."
Albert Camus

Much of the gratitude I talk about needs to be centered in what I do with today. I consciously focus on the present, rather than procrastinating for the future. As a sick alcoholic, I either lived in the guilt of yesterday or the fear of tomorrow. I missed the reality of the present.

The present moment is all I have. Through this moment, I live, breathe, and have my existence! My understanding of prayer is centered in the present moment because any understanding of relationship and communication, especially with God, must begin from where I am, rather than where I would like to be. Spirituality is the reality of the moment.

Spirit of the universe, thank You
for the life I experience in the moment.

Principles

"Nothing can bring you peace but the triumph of principles."
Ralph Waldo Emerson

I am beginning to understand what principles mean in my life. I am learning to live by a code of ethics I do not always like but know is good for me and others. Although I do not always fully understand the spiritual principles of life, I know my ongoing recovery should be based upon them.

Some of the spiritual principles by which I try to live are Honesty, Truth, Openness, Forgiveness, Acceptance, Humility, and Hope. I experience personal satisfaction knowing I live with principles that work. I am beginning to feel what I always thought other people had. Today I am alive in my life.

May Your principles be my lifestyle.

Suffering

"Every person, on the foundation of his or her own sufferings and joys, builds for all."
Albert Camus

In my pain, I am able to reach out to others. When I share my pain, I not only understand but I am understood.

Sometimes, it is my pain and suffering that unite me with others. Other people become a part of my life and are involved in who I am.

Through my shared feelings, other people begin to share. Trust develops across this bridge of understanding. Feelings unite the world.

Loving God, You created us in oneness.
Help me in my struggle to unite.

Reality

"I tend to be suspicious of people whose love of animals is exaggerated; they are often frustrated in their relationship with humans."
Yila (Camilla Koffler)

Anything can be used to avoid reality. People may use alcohol, food, drugs, people, sex, and gambling to avoid dealing with feelings.

The key to my addiction is in the obsessive and compulsive behavior patterns that stop me from reaching my full potential. I could not relax with who I was because of my exaggerated and painful lifestyle. I could not truly love myself because of my obsession with the "it" that seemed to be controlling me. At some point, I saw the obsession and began to talk about it.

For me to be a spiritual person, I must free myself from compulsive attitudes.

Dear God, may I meditate
on the comfort of freedom.

Life

"May you live all the days of your life."
Jonathan Swift

This story offers a key to the meaning of spirituality: Two little fish were huddled together, afraid to move. A large fish swam by them, confident and strong. The big fish shouted out, "Why don't you swim out and enjoy the beautiful ocean?" The two little fish looked at each other and asked, "What ocean?" They were in it, but they were unaware.

As an alcoholic, I existed in life but I did not live. I missed people, friendships, feelings, nature, and God. Like many addicts, I was among the "walking dead." Today I continue to make a spiritual choice that avoids alcohol. I am now able to feel again. I am alive.

In You, I live to love and love to live.

Solitude

"People who take time to be alone usually have depth, originality, and quiet reserve."
John Miller

Sometimes, I need to be alone. I need time to listen to my thoughts, consider my opinions, and strengthen my body. I need to pull away from my hectic life to be alone with me.

As a drinking alcoholic, I hated to be alone. I became paranoid about "leaving the fort." Today I accept that nobody is indispensable, and the world will still be there when I return from the desert!

I grow in the stillness of solitude. I can rest in that "still" part of me that is my essential self. God is very close to me in the silence.

God, in the stillness of Your life,
I am healed and rejuvenated.

Laughter

"You grow up the day you have the first real laugh—at yourself."
Ethel Barrymore

Today I can laugh at myself. I do not take myself too seriously. I am beginning to grow. I used to be too serious—having the "poor me" syndrome and sitting on my pity pot demanding attention. Not only was I terribly unhappy; I was the cause of my unhappiness.

One day, a friend listened to my complaints, then began to laugh a real belly laugh. Soon, I began to laugh, too! My attitude was so stupid, selfish, and futile that it demanded laughter to shake me out of it. At that point, I began to grow.

Now I laugh at my funny little ways, my ridiculous pretensions, and my grandiose behavior. With laughter comes humility.

God, let me experience the miracle of laughter.

Power

"Power does not corrupt. Fear corrupts, perhaps the fear of loss of power."
John Steinbeck

I now see that much of what we perceive as power in the world is really fear. Power that seeks to attack first to feel secure is fear. Power that always demands an answer is fear. Power that arrogantly refuses to listen is fear.

Spiritual power can be vulnerable. It can live with confusion. It can stand alone. It allows others to walk away to pursue their own happiness. Spiritual power can exist in suffering and loneliness and does not expect perfection.

My recovery is teaching me to live and let others live, too. My freedom must respect the freedom of others. Respect is a two-way street.

Give me the power that can rest in imperfection.

God

"Any God I ever felt in Church I brought in with me. And I think all the other folks did, too. They come to Church to share God, not find God."
Alice Walker

I used to think God was separate, unknowable, and judgmental. I saw God more as a judge than a friend and myself more as a sinner than the son. With such low self-esteem, it was hard to associate God with my life!

Then I began to search for the spiritual path to a deeper understanding of self. I found a loving, friendly God whose love is so pervasive I was able to discover the Divine in my life and the lives of others. The concept of meeting together to share God made sense. Discovering a God within made God knowable and comprehensible. Because God lives in me, I am alive.

Loving Creator, may I share
Your life in my world.

Freedom

"Without the possibility of choice and the exercise of choice one is not a person but a member, an instrument, a thing."
Archibald MacLeish

Spirituality involves the freedom to change. Growth requires a variety of choices. My past addiction was a life of slavery because it removed my creative choice and left me obsessing about drugs and alcohol. My life, conversation, and thoughts revolved around the bottle, and I was oblivious to the true meaning of life.

My freedom to experience the spiritual power of God's creativity was lost in the mindless craving for drugs. In this sense, drug addiction is slavery.

Today I am free to see God's world in people, places, and things. Now I make the choice to live, love, and laugh.

I am growing in my awareness of
Your multifaceted love for me.

Change

"There is nothing permanent except change."
Heraclitus

I know I need to change. My past behaviors and attitudes were negative and destructive. Today I choose to work on my addiction. I was changing before I embraced a spiritual program, but for the worse. Each day I grew more dependent, isolated, angry, and depressed. I felt I was a hopeless case!

Now I am working on my anger and loneliness. I talk about my pain and distress. I express my resentments and fears—and life is getting better. God created the world in perpetual change, and I believe God may be discovered in that change. I am evolving into Truth with my steps toward recovery—this is my "Yes" to God.

In the daily changes I discover Your stability.

Values

*"A person who dares to waste one hour of time
has not discovered the value of life."*
Charles Darwin

Life is not to be wasted. Time is not to be wasted. Friends, relationships, and opportunities are not to be wasted. Why? Because as a vulnerable human being, I do not have ultimate control. I do not know when my life will end, when I shall die, or when time and opportunity will be no more! Life is too precious to waste.

As an addict, I did not value life or time. I did not value friends or relationships. Nothing was valued except the alcohol! My life was meaningless. God was absent, and I felt nothing.

Today this is not the case. Through my pain, I have found the value of life and discovered a God of my understanding.

God, let me value what I have while I have it.

Music

"Sorrow, gladness, yearning, hope, and love belong to all of us, in all times and in all places. Music is the only means whereby we feel these emotions in their universality."

H. A. Overstreet

Music is a language for the world. It unites people, cultures, and religions. Music points people beyond themselves, while at the same time breathing God's glory through them. Music makes us wonder, enables us to dream, and allows us to rest in the miracle of creativity.

Drugs stopped me from appreciating the music. They corrupted sounds and made them destructive. Drugs left me with a feeling of utter emptiness.

In recovery, I can hear again. My spiritual program incorporates music—different types of music and the inexhaustible joys of melody. I feel in it, through it, with it—another miracle.

Thank You for the gift of music that enables me to grow in understanding.

Divinity

"To say we are made up of certain chemical elements is a satisfactory description only for those who intend to use us as fertilizer."
Herbert J. Muller

Humans are more than chemicals. Human beings carry the image of God, the imprint of Divinity, and the power of the Creative Spirit.

As an addict, I doubted myself, thereby adding to my powerlessness and unmanageability. Internally I said, "I can't," even before I tried. My low self-esteem was evident long before I took a drink. I tried to match my "outsides" to what I imagined your "insides" to be like.

When I accepted my alcoholism, I was able to discover God in my life. Today I create through God and in God. Spirituality comes with the awareness of my God-given Divinity.

May I never cease to recognize You in my life.

Humankind

"Humankind is what it believes."
Anton Chekhov

My miracle is that I now believe in me. I accept my addiction and do not resist or deny it. I believe I am an alcoholic, an overeater, a codependent, or an adult child of an alcoholic. My belief sets me free.

For too long, I played the game of control, blaming, and bargaining—and I lost. I now surrender to the reality of who I am. I accept my disease and make choices based on my awareness. And it is getting better.

My belief about addiction gives me insight into God and freedom. God loves me enough to give me choice, and with it comes responsibility. I am responsible for how I live with my addictions. Today I accept that responsibility.

What I believe reflects the God
I believe in. I believe in You.

Imperfection

"In the country of the blind a one-eyed king can still goof up."
Anonymous

For years I tried to control everything and everybody. There was a correct code of behavior, and everything had its place. I felt responsible for the universe and everyone in it.

Today I can laugh at my mistakes and the mistakes of others. When I catch myself organizing the world, I remember where the "perfect" yesterdays got me—and I laugh. God made me with a navel and flat feet; I would have preferred something different, but there is a loving message in my imperfections—it is okay to goof up! I relax in the humor of being human.

Thank You for making me an angel in the dirt.

Answers

"If the work of God could be comprehended by reason, it would be no longer wonderful, and faith would have no merit if reason provided proof."
Pope Gregory I

Some things happen that I do not comprehend, but I have faith they will happen again tomorrow: sunsets, night following day, birds singing, the colors of nature, and the joy of being alive. Perhaps the biggest mystery for humankind is love. People may suffer, endure persecution, and even be put to death for something they love. The pain and sorrow of love are mingled into being human.

Reason does not have the answers to life. Faith is the medication for our existence. We have a belief in tomorrow because of what we have experienced today. If I can say no to alcohol today, then I can do it again tomorrow —if I really want to.

God, let me not seek proof but the willingness to grapple with the problems of life.

Religion

"All religions must be tolerated . . . for . . . every-one must get to heaven his or her own way."
Frederick the Great

There are many ways to God, and I believe Christianity is one way. However, I am convinced there are other ways with or without religion. My experience of the Church has been good. I have been encouraged to question and doubt, search for new areas of faith within my agnosticism, and explore other religions. My experience of Christianity has been supportive of openness and compassion.

God is not a prisoner of any religion. We can all learn from each other's experiences, but we need to listen. To dismiss arrogantly the value a religion can bring is as negative and sick as accepting what a religion says without question.

Let me find in the religions of the world
the oneness of Your truth.

Prejudice

"It is never too late to give up your prejudices."
Henry David Thoreau

Prejudice divides people and feeds on anger, resentment, and fear. Today I realize my prejudices stemmed from seeing in others what I disliked in myself. I hated people who appeared weak and vulnerable because I was weak and vulnerable. I hated people who stood up for their principles and talked about their feelings because, as a drunk, I never really had any principles, and I could not get in touch with my feelings.

Now I try to talk about my prejudices and overcome them. Knowledge of those people I disliked has proven useful in slowly overcoming my prejudices.

Teach me to locate myself
in my criticism of others.

Enjoyment

"Humankind, unlike animals, has never learned the sole purpose of life is to enjoy it."
Samuel Butler

Spirituality enables me to enjoy my life. I enjoy my sobriety. I enjoy the freedom of a God of my understanding. I enjoy the sharing of ideas and opinions based on love and honesty. The world is to be enjoyed and not endured! God is fun.

For years, I thought God was a judge to be feared—angry, hostile, and vengeful. Strange how silly this all seems now, but for years I was afraid of God and feared God's presence. Then I was introduced to a God who is beyond institutions and dogma, free of creeds and punishment, a loving and joyous God who created me to be happy. Today I am enjoying my freedom.

God, Creator of the Universe,
You are parent to us all.

Originality

"Originality does not consist in saying what no one has ever said before, but in saying exactly what you think yourself."
James Stephens

Sometimes I surprise myself with what I say, think, or contemplate. Within my being is a very strange world I wish to share with others.

If I am truly honest about what I think and feel, it may unite me with the true identity of others. Perhaps we are all a little strange! However, I will never know what people are thinking or feeling unless I take a risk and share myself honestly.

My involvement with my fellow and sister humans revolves around honesty. Today I am willing to speak my truth.

In the knowledge of Your love,
let me share my feelings.

May

Scripture

"Nobody ever outgrows Scripture; the book widens and deepens with our years."
Charles Haddan Spurgeon

Not so long ago, I held a rigid religious outlook based solely on my narrow belief system. I was addicted to my religious approach and any alternative or variation was condemned prior to investigation. I was a religious bigot. I was a hypocrite. I hid behind dogma and ritual.

Today I have a comprehensive view of religion and God, thanks to the influence of recovering alcoholics and the discovery of a spiritual program. I am able to see the depth and richness of scripture, a living library of books and experiences. I am able to see beyond the printed word to the message of healing and love that comes with honesty and acceptance.

Wind of Truth, continue to blow
and inspire me through apparent difference.

Facts

*"Facts do not cease to exist because they are
ignored."*
Aldous Huxley

Reality is not dependent upon acceptance. Addiction does not have to be accepted to be real. Alcoholism was killing people long before it had a name!

A big part of my life was spent denying I had a problem. My manipulative art was exercised in discovering more acceptable excuses for my drunkenness, rather than looking at the problem. Belief in the God of truth did not stop my dishonesty.

The process of self-love and acceptance began in my cry for help. Surrender brought me sanity. God's purpose is being worked out in my life because I am finally getting out of my own way. I am facing the facts.

Help me to never ignore what I know to be true.

Uniqueness

"God sees nothing as average."
Anonymous

God created every human being from the dust and bestowed upon all of us the Divine Image. This means I, too, am Divine. I am a creature created to create. I share God's love for the universe. I am anything but average!

For years I thought I was not good enough. I needed alcohol, drugs, food, or people to make me okay. I considered myself less than, inferior, and a freak.

Today I awaken to a new message. The spiritual message tells me I am forever holding God's hand. God needs you and me to work in the divine vineyard. In us, God makes miracles. I know I am beautiful, important, and unique.

Help me be healed daily by beholding
my own beauty within and without.

War

"War is only a cowardly escape from the problems of peace."
Thomas Mann

Sometimes it is easier to attack than discuss and seek harmony. It is easier to lash out, hurt, maim, or destroy than listen, forgive, understand, and reconcile. Violence is often the cowardly way out.

The sadness for society is that war and violence are often presented as heroic. Our modern heroes often carry weapons rather than the olive branch. Surrender is seen as cowardice. Gentleness is seen as weakness. The diplomat is seen as the schemer.

My recovery teaches me that nothing is gained by acts of violence. In the atmosphere of peace, God and humankind can be reconciled.

Give me the courage to surrender on a daily basis and bring harmony into my world.

Hope

"Hope is the pillar that holds up the world."
Pliny the Elder

When I look at the world, I discover an order and a pattern to life, a balance within the system. I do not believe in a God of chaos. I find a spiritual stability in creation. Night follows day. Death makes way for life. People, regardless of culture or creed, are remarkably similar in feelings and needs. The God who created this world has given seeds of hope to the living.

I am the key to the understanding of the universe. In this observation I find hope. When I go with the flow of life, I find peace and stability. It is only when I fight the system that I experience pain.

God of order and stability, bring balance into my life through the spiritual changes I make.

Childlike

"In every real person a child is hidden that wants to play."

Friedrich Nietzsche

Having a spiritual program means I can play and have fun. I am a mature adult, and I can still enjoy the swings in the park. But, more important, I have a daily sense of adventure. My eyes light up as I ask How? When? Where? These words still dominate my life.

I am excited about life. I am excited about my life. God is forever present in this world of color, movement, and change. But for me, God is most clearly seen in people. Others are a constant fascination. Part of my play involves people-watching, and as I gaze, my mouth still opens in amazement. The child in me fully enjoys the world in which I play.

Thank You for the toys, people, and differences that add color to my world.

Success

"There is no failure except in no longer trying."
Elbert Hubbard

I produced the failure in my life. For years, I blamed everything and everyone: parents, job, health, income, a cruel world, thoughtless friends, and the weather!

Today I own my failures because they are mine. I also see my successes, and this makes me a winner. I see the things I have achieved, the character defects I have confronted, and the happiness that comes with an acceptance of self.

I may not be perfect, but I am certainly not worthless. I may make mistakes, but I am not evil. I have a heart that needs to love and also needs to be loved. I am willing to reveal my vulnerability and discover its strength.

*May I continue to seek Your power
and glory in my life.*

Honesty

"Where is there dignity unless there is honesty?"
Marcus Tullius Cicero

Honesty is the cornerstone of my life. It is the quality I most desire because it brings knowledge of God, self, and relationships. Honesty is key to my recovery from addiction.

As an alcoholic, I was dishonest—not only because I told lies and manipulated the truth but also because I refused to risk the journey into self. My dishonesty was not about what I said or did but what I failed to say or do. It stopped me from discovering my God-given dignity.

Today I risk the journey into self. I discover more about God as I become willing to understand God. Honesty helps me be happy and relaxed with who I am.

In the silence of self-honesty, may I know myself.

Poetry

"Poetry is the rhythmical creation of beauty in words."

Edgar Allan Poe

Language helps us understand and communicate. Poetry adds the dimensions of shape and movement. Poetry seems to go beyond words and ideas to the very essence of what life is about. It hints at Divinity!

When I was drinking, I never understood the value of poetry. Today I use poetry as part of my adventure into meaning and self-knowledge.

So much more is open to me in sobriety, and I am able to appreciate things I never used to comprehend. Poetry is part of "It gets better."

May I seek You in all aspects of art.

Creativity

"When one is painting, one does not think."
Raphael Sanzio

Artists are predominantly people who feel rather than think; they are molding their most inner experiences into the finished product.

I am doing the same in my sobriety. I am molding something good and wholesome from a life that was negative and destructive. I am rediscovering God not just in thoughts and ideas but in the daily happenings of my life.

God is alive in my relationships, behavior, and daily acts of kindness. God is a process in which I am involved. God is at the center of my life, regardless of the ordinariness of the event. Art is part of my life because I am a creative human being.

Teach me to look beyond the painting into myself.

Procrastination

"Procrastination—the art of keeping up with yesterday."
Don Marquis

As a drinking alcoholic, my life was littered with promises never kept and intentions never honored. I pushed everything into tomorrow, and tomorrow never came.

Now I try to do all I have set for myself to do in a given day. I make a list of things I need and want to do. The things I need to do usually take priority.

When I awake, I thank God for my sleep. I make a silent intention not to drink today; then I face my responsibilities. I separate "needs" from "wants." I remember my responsibility to family, friends, and colleagues. I am learning to live in my day.

God, may I do the things I should do, and may I find time for the things I want to do.

Responsibility

"We must cease attributing our problems to our environment and learn again to exercise our will, our personal responsibility in the realm of faith and morals."
Albert Schweitzer

God created me to be a responsible human being. I must seriously consider the choices and decisions that affect my life and the lives of others. Today I understand true freedom can only be experienced within the parameters of a responsible life.

For years I blamed other people for my drunken behavior, but the truth was I lived an irresponsible life around alcohol. I ignored the facts that surrounded my drinking. Now I make the decision to not drink. I also take responsibility for my life. I cannot blame other people for the mistakes I made. My real freedom is experienced in responsibility.

*Give me the freedom to impose
my own boundaries.*

Arguments

"Argument is the worst sort of conversation."
Jonathan Swift

Why did I argue so much? Why do I argue so much? Usually, it is because I feel threatened, angry, discounted, or I am wrong and do not want to admit it.

Today I remember healthy discussion is the better path to follow. I need to hear and understand what the other person is saying and to try to see from his or her point of view.

Arguments hurt others and me. My program today allows my ego to be balanced and restrained. I try to think before I speak. I consider before I react. And, when I do get into arguments and say hurtful and painful things, I am brave enough to say I am sorry.

God of peace, love, and acceptance,
may You be seen in my relationships.

Sex

"A little theory makes sex more interesting, more comprehensive, and less scary."
Alex Comfort

Sometimes, we make too much of sex because we are afraid of it. We abuse God's gift of sex by placing it out of context, removing it from other things that make it meaningful, such as gentleness, trust, sensitivity, communication, and commitment.

When performance becomes more important than expression, meaning gets lost in the process. In such instances, God's precious gift of sex is abused by the act itself. Compulsive sex is merely demonstrated loneliness!

Spirituality teaches me to see all things as part of God's gift of wholeness. Sex is an important part of this—but only a part.

In the awareness of sexuality, may I discover a relationship with myself, others, and You.

Teaching

"To teach is to learn."
Japanese Proverb

The more I learn the more I realize there is much I do not understand. Life is full of wonderful information. Paradoxes and confusion abound. Every new idea leads to a further truth, and the journey seems endless.

In a sense, we are all disciples. We are all learning from each other, and the roles of teacher and student are forever being exchanged. In sobriety, I see how many wonderful phenomena exist in the world: so many fascinating and interesting places to visit, so many loving and insightful people to get to know. God has given me so much. I am deeply grateful for the opportunity to learn in God's garden.

Teacher, may I never stop learning
and being a student in Your world.

Liberty

"Liberty means responsibility. That is why most people dread it."
George Bernard Shaw

The fellowship of recovering addicts and their families rejoice in the freedom of life, the exchange of slavery to a substance or person for liberty and a life of choice rather than meaningless compulsion. And, with the gift of liberty comes the weight of responsibility.

Today I am responsible for my life. I can no longer say I do not know. I cannot continue to blame others for my disease or manipulate my way through the playground of denial.

My spiritual program requires a maturity of lifestyle that involves responsibility—and the joys are immense!

Creator of liberty and responsibility,
let me not forget to laugh.

Tolerance

"Tolerance is the positive and cordial effort to understand another's beliefs, practices, and habits without necessarily sharing or accepting them."
Joshua Liebman

I am happy to tolerate others. I listen to what they say and, if I do not agree, it is okay! I do not have to agree with people to accept and befriend them.

This is a new attitude for me. It is a crucial part of my spiritual program. When I was drinking, I did not listen to people whose ideas were different from mine. I would not tolerate those who had a different philosophy of life. I discounted other religions, regarding them as cultlike, crude, or superstitious.

Today I learn from people who view God, the world, and morality differently. Spirituality is teaching me to be open and accepting.

God, may I find traces of Your love in different philosophies and religions.

Faith

"Faith has need of the whole truth."
Pierre Teilhard de Chardin

Faith is a journey that begins and ends in God. Understanding imperfection teaches me to look beyond myself to a truth yet to be revealed. Daily attitude adjustments bring me to truth and freedom.

Today it is sufficient to know I am not God. The hardest part of being human is accepting the limitations of my life. Things happen without my involvement. I need not be there for existence to happen; there is life beyond me!

I do not hold the world together; God does. Truth is in me but also beyond me. In this sense, my faith is enriched by others.

As I look to the future,
I see Your oneness in tomorrow.

Money

"Money is the symbol of duty. It is the sacrament of having done for humankind that which humankind wanted."
Samuel Butler

How people pay us for services we perform is symbolic of our value. In this society, money is also a force behind much creativity and job satisfaction. The danger is in becoming a snob—thinking we are better than others because we earn more income.

My spirituality is about discovering the oneness of humankind and incorporating our creative differences. We can all learn from each other. Any sign of pretentiousness is indicative of insecurities that need to be dealt with within my recovery program.

God, let my gratitude be seen in my relationship with money and with others.

Religion

"You have not converted a person because you have silenced them."
Viscount John Morley

I cannot force someone into faith. I cannot make someone believe. I cannot bribe a person into prayer. So much of my early religion was about making a deal: You do this and you will get this. If you do this for God and the Church, you will be happy and successful. There always seemed to be a payoff with God.

I think much of the silent majority senses the same kind of thing: God has gotten lost in the business of religion. Spirituality accepts the pain, confusion, and anger of this silent majority and says, "Find a God of your own understanding." When you discover your power in life, God will be perceived.

God, in my silence is the shout heard.

Art

"Art flourishes where there is a sense of adventure."
Alfred North Whitehead

I enjoy and am sustained by life and the adventure of living. For years, I spent my time avoiding situations, avoiding people, and avoiding me.

Now in my daily recovery, I need to participate and experience my spiritual energy. I want to meet new people. I want to travel. I want to work productively and earn money. I want to add something to this beautiful world.

I am discovering that my experience of creative spirituality makes me an artist. God is found in the hugs I share and the early-morning "hellos" I shout to strangers. I am not afraid anymore. Today I am alive.

God, let me find You in the small matters
of life; let me find You where I am.

Earth

"This could be such a beautiful world."
Rosalind Welcher

The beauty I see in the world also reveals sadness—
sadness in knowing it could be a much more loving and
accepting place for everybody. If only we would get together
in our differences instead of demanding sameness.

We destroy so much God-given beauty by our desire
to control, understand, and arrogantly pursue a philosophy of selfishness—and we all lose.

My spiritual hope for tomorrow comes in the creative
choices I make today.

Let me be a good steward in
Your world because it is Your gift to all.

Effort

"Do what you can, with what you have, where you are."
Theodore Roosevelt

I am not perfect, but I can still do my best. Because my recovery is an ongoing process, my best is improving on a daily basis. It is so easy to beat myself up emotionally by thinking my best is not good enough. Even after time in recovery, I still sometimes hear the old tapes: Is that all you can do?

I need to remember the disease of addiction still lives in my recovery. However, my attempts at dealing with a problem or helping another with a problem will usually be more than sufficient. Today I accept my best attempts with gratitude, and I am not too proud to seek the advice of another.

God, accept the best I can offer
as an instrument of your peace.

Immaturity

"My mother loved children; she would have given anything if I had been one."
Groucho Marx

For too many years, I allowed myself to be treated as a child. I played the child role to avoid responsibility.

Part of my people-pleasing was living as a thirty-year-old child! I was afraid to say no, to disappoint, or to hurt another's feelings. I was afraid to tell my parents how they were hurting me by their need to control my life. I spent years feeling guilty and afraid.

I am willing to deal with this pain in my life. I am willing to talk about it. My biggest relief comes in knowing I am not alone. There are millions of us out there. The difference is I have a program that enables me to talk about what I need.

God, help me to be childlike without
being childish. Help me grow
to maturity with a smile.

Variety

"The growth of the human mind is still high adventure, in many ways the highest adventure on earth."
Norman Cousins

Today my life is an adventure. I am prepared for the unusual. I expect the confusion of life. I revel in God's reflected difference within creation—variety and my acceptance of it are part of my joy in living.

I find God in the seemingly ordinary things in life: dance, relationships, old movies, jogging, my dog, and sincere hugs. The adventure I find in life reflects my adventure in God.

Spirituality is seeing beyond the ordinary into the extraordinary: The Kingdom of God is within.

*May I always find You
in the smallest and strangest of places.*

Space

"That's one small step for man, one giant leap for mankind."

Neil A. Armstrong

There is no end to what people can achieve when they behave responsibly and honestly, working with others to discover more about themselves and the universe. God made us in the Divine image with all the power and creativity that implies. The dangers that forever surround humankind are greed, pride, and the misuse of power.

As a recovering alcoholic, I understand this only too well. Ego made me arrogant and selfish. If this is true for me and for others, it must also be true for governments, countries, and alliances. Countries do not make wars—people do. Our universe must be seen as belonging to everyone—or it will belong to no one!

Let me learn to enjoy and share
Your garden and not destroy it.

Motives

"Lord, grant that I may always desire more than I can accomplish."
Michelangelo

I must always think big, not in an egotistical sense but as an adventure in spirituality. When I had a small God, I remained a small person with small aspirations and dreams. Today I have an all-embracing, inclusive God that fills the universe. I have hope in my dreams.

As an alcoholic, I missed so much. I observed very little about myself and God's world. Nothing really mattered except my desire to drink. Now I realize my potential and know I can risk in sobriety. My motto has become "Go for it." Behind my dreams is my growth. I have a sense of so much joy in the world that I wish to enthusiastically experience my life.

God, I am so grateful to be alive.

Christianity

"One who begins by loving Christianity better than Truth will proceed by loving one's church better than Christianity, and end in loving oneself better than all."
Samuel Taylor Coleridge

My program of recovery is spiritual and not religious. Spirituality encompasses all that is good and noble in all the religions of the world. It cannot be confined within or limited to one religion or denomination.

Spirituality stops the recovering person from looking for differences. Spiritual practice puts an end to arrogance and prejudice that feed the disease of addiction. God is revealed in the multitudes of the universe. I find God in the sunset, the variety of animals, the love and care of family and friends, the excitement and vision of poetry and art, and the inspiration of music. Spirituality is all this and more!

Kneeling before the beauty of Your creation, I whisper, "Amen."

Self

"The fault, dear Brutus, is not in the stars, but in ourselves, that we are underlings."
William Shakespeare

My addiction to alcohol led me away from self. Today in sobriety, I am beginning to understand me.

For years, I blamed others for my misfortunes, but now I see I was the enemy in my life. It was a cop-out to blame God, family, job, or life for my alcoholism; I needed to take responsibility for myself.

Part of my recovery program involves not looking outside for answers but looking within. The answer is not in the stars, not in fate, but rather in the destiny I create by the decisions I make today. I and I alone forge my future.

God, let me create a life that
is pleasing in Your sight.

Posterity

*"We need to make a world in which fewer chil-
dren are born, and in which we take better care
of them."*
George Wald, M.D.

Spirituality is concerned with the physical. How I
exercise and develop a healthy food plan is as important as prayer, reading, and meditation. The body is part
of the soul.

I also have a responsibility for the future, for those
who follow me on this planet. The ecological welfare of
this world is spiritual. An irresponsibility concerning
childbirth reveals an arrogance that does not belong to
the spiritual program. The satisfaction of my personal
desires should never hurt the lives of others—including
the unborn.

*Teach me to have a spiritual
responsibility to the future.*

Ambition

"Show me a thoroughly satisfied individual and I will show you a failure."
Thomas Alva Edison

I need to strive for new things in my life. I need to push out into new areas and discover the richness of God's world. I need to explore the varied beauty of creation.

There is so much I have not done because of the years of my addiction. So much I have not seen, countries I have not visited, languages I have not learned, and experiences I have missed. My compulsive and obsessive behavior left me a prisoner and a victim of self.

The spiritual recovery I enjoy today says it is okay for me to have things, enjoy things, and do things.

Help me realize the energy and ambition
You have created within me.

June

Aging

"Old age is when you realize other people's faults are no worse than your own."
Edgar Shoaff

I am on a journey to God that includes many stages of experience—good and bad, painful and joyful, confusing and clear. These experiences will take me into a period of life called "old age."

I feared the aging process because it has been associated with poor health, helplessness, and death. The uncertainty of death brought a lack of control. Guilt and fear of God were also involved.

We all have similar fears and concerns. Mystery brings a sense of awe! Today I have a loving God that is involved in my life. In my recovery, I have a better perspective on life. Age brings balance.

*Thank You for the balance
that comes with personal forgiveness.*

Time

"Everything one does enough of eventually generates its own interest and one then begins to believe in it."
Alan Dunn

I never thought I could stay sober. For years I tried to abstain with no success. It was not stopping that was difficult, for I could stop three times in one week! Staying stopped was the challenge.

Then somebody said, "Try stopping for twenty-four hours. If that proves too long, try stopping until the morning or for one hour or even one minute. If the cravings get too severe, call me, but don't take that first drink!"

My abstinence began in periods of twenty-four hours. Life is made up of days, and I live one day at a time. I am successful. I have built time in sobriety based on the simple maxim "Don't drink today." I believe in it. I believe in me. And it gets better.

Creator of time, thank You
for the simplicity of days, hours, and minutes.

Dreams

"I like the dreams of the future better than the history of the past."
Thomas Jefferson

I am an optimist. I believe things are getting better day by day. I believe what happened yesterday need not happen today or tomorrow. Dreams can come true. I know this to be a fact.

I have dreams. I have hope for my life, and on a daily basis it is coming true. My life is becoming more meaningful. My dreams have coincided with God's dream for me.

I love myself enough to speak out for me, and it feels good. Now my decision to embrace the spiritual life is not dependent upon others. Today I can dream to be me.

Help me dream with my feet
firmly on the ground.

Profit

"What is one to profit if one shall gain the whole world and lose one's own soul?"
Matthew 16:26

Spirituality brings a sense of priority to my life: First things first. Unless I discover me and have a love and respect for myself, I have nothing to offer in this world.

I am the center of my universe, and through my life God is radiated. I am part of God's creative plan, and the pleasures of this world are secondary to developing a right relationship with God.

My disease of obsession and compulsion wants me to focus on other things: food, alcohol, drugs, people, money, success, or ego. My program reminds me my love of self is shown in my refusal of the first drink. If I am healthy, I can have the world; without me, I have nothing!

Let me find Your Kingdom within.

Reason

"I do not feel obliged to believe the same God who has endowed us with sense, reason, and intellect has intended us to forego their use."
Galileo Galilei

An essential part of being human is the ability to think, reflect, and reason. Spirituality is involved in our ideas and perceptions because that is historically how humankind has grown and been able to change. As Descartes so aptly put it, "Cogito ergo sum"—I think, therefore I am.

The tragedy is that few people experience the freedom to think and create because of the stifling addictions that are epidemic in our society: food, alcohol, drugs, religion, work, money, and sex. We are so afraid of what others might think or say that we never fully experience our spiritual selves, and everybody suffers. Ironically, it is the risk in life that makes people great.

Help me challenge what I do not believe
to discover what I do believe.

Science

"As long as humans are free to ask what they must, free to say what they think, free to think what they will, freedom can never be lost and science can never regress."
Robert Oppenheimer

I need to press on in this wonderful journey of life because new discoveries await me in my tomorrows. Spirituality always brings joy in the journey. In the traveling is the fun, for I will never reach my destination in this life.

The freedom to question is part of the discipline of science, and science is involved in the treatment and recovery of addiction. We must always be looking for better ways of treatment, more vivid ways of teaching, and creative aids to recovery.

Science, and every other creative discipline, should be used in the treatment of addictions. God is to be found in the many.

Creator, let me remember you gave humankind a scalpel and a prayer book.

Greed

"One of the weaknesses of our age is our apparent inability to distinguish our needs from our greeds."
Don Robinson

I was a greedy drunk and a greedy person—spoiled, selfish, and demanding. I felt the world owed me a living, and if I did not get my way, I sulked, cried, or tried to hurt people. This greedy attitude toward life only made me sad, dull, and boring. Greed, in this sense, could not work because what I was craving would never satisfy me.

Then I learned to let go. Instead of demanding, I learned to wait. Instead of consuming alcohol, I practiced abstinence. Instead of expecting life on my terms, I went with the natural flow of life. I am happy, joyous, and free. A miracle? Yes. I accepted my needs, and with acceptance came satisfaction.

God, only when I accept my hunger
for You am I truly satisfied.

Doubt

"I respect faith, but doubt is what gets you an education."
Wilson Mizner

It is okay to question. It is okay to say I do not agree. I have the freedom to doubt opinions and attitudes.

In childhood, I was never allowed to question. I had to accept the Bible because the preacher said it was God's word. I had to believe only Christians went to Heaven because Grandma said so! I had to agree so-called social minorities were inferior because family and friends said so. To doubt any of this was to be different.

Then I learned growth comes to those who are prepared to doubt or disagree with an existing system. God is found in questions. Spirituality is discovered in the shades of life.

God, part of Your glory and splendor
is Your unending mystery.

Ideals

"Every dogma has its day, but ideals are eternal."
Israel Zangwill

For too long, I lived in a box of rules and dogma. Life had to have answers and structure. Eventually, the answers did not work. Nobody was interested in my answers. The world had moved on!

I realized life had to be lived, not simply talked about. Having the answers to questions no one—including me—was asking seemed a waste of time. I was living in the past.

Spirituality is reality. It is okay to benefit from a tradition, then move on. I was not disloyal because I changed my mind. God and truth live in a changing world, and if I am to grow, my perception of myself and life must change. Today I can accept this.

God, give me the willingness
to change in my life.

Laughter

"God cannot be solemn, or God would not have blessed humankind with the incalculable gift of laughter."
Sydney Harris

The way to understand God is to begin to understand people! Sometimes I forget I bear the image of God. This is not so much physical as emotional; it is my inner self, my soul. I believe what I feel, what hurts me, and what causes me distress and pain also affects God.

The gifts of creative intelligence and spiritual sacrifice that have characterized many people in history reflect something of God. Laughter is involved in this. Laughter is divinely derived and is part of the spiritual gift God has bequeathed to every one of us; I need only discover it. Let go and let God. Sometimes I need to get out of my own way so I can begin to laugh.

God, you gave the gift of laughter to be used.
May I use it in the precious art of healing.

Solitude

"Everyone should try to find a spot to be alone."
Queen Juliana

Greta Garbo is often quoted as having said "I want to be alone." Life brings pressures, and we all need to find a place where we can be alone.

I need time alone not to think or do but to simply be. I need time to rest. I need a time in the day I can call my own, to have a visit with the most important person in my life—me!

To rest in self is to experience spiritual "self-ish-ness"— the joy of self-love.

Today I look forward to setting aside time just for my heart and mind to center on the pathway, listening to God.

Sometimes, I need to be alone.
In that peace, I unite with You.

Potential

"There is no meaning to life except the meaning one gives life by the unfolding of one's powers."
Eric Fromm

I was powerless when I was drinking. Alcohol kept me from reaching my full potential. I was depressed, tired, angry, lonely, and confused. I was the enemy in my life. By drinking alcohol, I fed the disease and made my life unmanageable.

Then I had a "moment" in which I saw what I was doing to my life. The pain caused by drinking outweighed any advantages. I had hit my bottom.

I began to change by refusing the first drink; then I began to experience a new vitality and potential. Friendships and relationships were possible again. God became understandable. My power as a human being is unleashed in sobriety.

*God, may I discover my potential
in the loving decisions I make.*

World

"We are citizens of the world, and the tragedy of our time is that we do not know this."
Woodrow Wilson

In recovery I have learned to "go home" to who I am. This involves understanding my place in the universe. I am a child of God. My "family" does not merely consist of blood relatives; it includes the millions of other people who inhabit this planet.

God did not make only me. God does not love only me. God is concerned for all people. As a practicing alcoholic, I did not have this healthy attitude. I felt lost and different. I became selfish and narrow in my lifestyle.

Today I have a big God who enables me to grow in my acceptance of self and others. I am a citizen of the world, and it feels good.

God, may I always know what it means
to belong to the human family.

Life

"To be free is to have achieved your life."
Tennessee Williams

Yesterday's tapes included thoughts like the following: I need a drink. I can't exist without a fix. How will I get through the morning? Do they see me shake? Are people watching? Where can I get money?

My addiction was a prison! Today I am free because I was courageous and asked for help. I am free because I still ask for help. I have learned to say no to the first drink, and life is more comfortable and less painful.

Freedom is a precious spiritual gift I work for on a daily basis. God is involved, and so am I. My freedom from alcoholism is only guaranteed by the creative choices I make.

God, my memory is the key to today's freedom.
May I continue to remember.

Fear

"Nothing is so much to be feared as fear."
Henry David Thoreau

Fear stops my God-given spirituality from taking shape. Fear is connected with doubt—more precisely, the doubt of self. Low self-esteem develops along with fear, and for confidence to develop, fear must be confronted and talked about.

Fear will not go away because I wish, hope, or pray it away. It must be located and seen for what it is and is not. Fear of people, things, tomorrow, or life itself grows when I forget I am a creature of God.

There is nothing I cannot face or overcome, as long as I remain drug free. God is on my side, but I also need to be on my side. Fear is never stronger than my spirituality.

Dear God, I ask to stay in the light of sobriety, not the darkness of alcoholism.

Learning

"Anyone who stops learning is old, whether at twenty or eighty. Anyone who keeps learning stays young. The greatest thing in life is to keep your mind young."
Henry Ford

My life is exciting because I am learning and creating so much in recovery. Even things I thought I understood have a new ring. Words, ideas, relationships, and the awareness of God are forever changing for the better.

My sobriety is not boring; it is not stuffy, rigid, or restrictive. My discussions (not arguments) within the fellowship of recovering people produce fresh insights.

Today I am involved in the life of God. I am creating, healing, and forever learning more about the mystery of love.

Teacher of the Universe,
let me seek beyond that which I understand.

Self-Love

"Only one who can live with oneself can enjoy the gift of leisure."
Henry Greber

As an addict, I could not tolerate my own company for long. I was forever phoning somebody, going to a friend's house, inviting people in, or creating occasions to not have to think about myself. Being alone terrified me because I did not want to face what was happening in my life.

Spirituality is reality. Some time ago, I decided to encounter the real me—painful but necessary. I began to develop an awareness of who I am. Acceptance followed: I am an alcoholic.

Today I know me. I like me and can even love me. My awareness brings knowledge of God, self, and neighbor. Today I can be alone without feeling lonely.

In Your presence, I begin to know myself.

Acceptance

"Less is more."
Mies van der Rohe

As a gambler, I always wanted more. I wanted to win more, have more, and spend more. My energy always focused on getting more, but the demanding lifestyle only brought me less.

I never stopped to smell the roses. Activity robbed me of satisfaction. I was running through my life and missing it. Then somebody told me to stop and rest. "Don't chase life; enjoy it!" was the admonition. Gambling was a compulsive and obsessive disease that was ruining my life.

Today I choose not to do this. I accept that the "less" in my life is giving me more. I take responsibility for me, and I share freely with other recovering gamblers.

God, teach me to see Your power
and beauty in what I am willing to give up.

Prejudice

*"A great many people think they are thinking
when they are only rearranging their prejudices."*
William James

An aspect of prejudice was my refusal to listen. I tended to stay with my own thinking and shut off people or ideas I did not want to hear. This attitude did not lead to discussion, growth, or change.

Spirituality is having the capacity to hear what others are saying. This includes people I may not like or respect. It means being prepared to live with and alongside confusion and difference. Truth is a many-sided diamond, and it cannot be comprehended from one viewpoint.

I need to remove my prejudices if I am ever to move toward an understanding of God's truth. I need to learn that the image of God is in every person I meet.

Teach me to listen so I may hear, so I may grow.

Thought

"Write down the thoughts of the moment. Those that come unsought are commonly the most valuable."

Francis Bacon

My mind sometimes races with ideas: What should I do? What should I write? Where should I go? The answers could prove useful.

Many of these ideas come late at night. Now I keep a note pad and a pencil beside my bed so I can write down the thought, then go back to sleep.

I am not God. I know that to say I will remember the thought tomorrow would be unrealistic. As an imperfect human being, I take any help I can get. The pad at the side of the bed is invaluable!

Let me employ discipline as an aid to joyful and creative living.

Lies

"The cruelest lies are often told in silence."
Robert Louis Stevenson

In treatment, I claimed I did not tell many lies. This was not true because it hid the fact that most of my lies were "lies of silence."

It was what I did not say that produced the confusion, the pretended self-confidence that hid my pain and shame, the half-spoken truth that harbored my disease.

Communication is the key to any spiritual relationship, and a sick silence creates the ultimate blasphemy. God created me to relate. In the interchange of ideas, a miracle is born. A sick, angry, and ego-centered silence is my shouted "No" to God.

Creator of paradox, let me see how lies
of silence can destroy my world.

Individuality

"You'll never really know what I mean, and I'll never really know exactly what you mean."
Mike Nichols

I am not always sure I know what I feel or think; as such, I cannot be sure of what anyone else feels or thinks. When I say "I know how you feel," it is with some reservation. Another challenge is finding words to express what I feel. Although words are bridges to meaning, they may also be barriers to understanding. What I mean by what I say is sometimes misunderstood.

Awareness inspires me to be more creative in communication. Today I consider more seriously what the other person means, rather than just listening to the words. Because I am sensitive to being understood, I am becoming patient with others.

*Teach me, God, never to become
a victim of my language.*

Reality

"Do not take life too seriously. You will never get out of it alive."
Elbert Hubbard

When I took life too seriously, I was miserable. I missed so much. I focused a disproportionate amount of energy on my own importance. I am not saying I am not important, but I must learn to live within the structures of this world.

For so long, I made myself the victim of the world. Every appointment I missed was seen as a personal abuse. I could not wait in line without getting angry and resentful toward everybody around. Others were expected to revolve around me, and I felt the world owed me a living!

I needed to change or remain unhappy. Today I am learning to change and I am working on patience.

Thank You for the spiritual gift
of balance in my life.

Perfection

"I have offended God and humankind because my work did not reach the quality it should have."
Leonardo da Vinci

How I used to beat myself up! I was not good enough or attractive enough. I could not speak properly. My family was not prestigious. I failed to appreciate my value. I could not see beyond my failings to my God-given virtues. Sin was all too evident in my experience!

Now I recognize egotism in my criticism of self and others! Who was I to think I should be perfect? My compulsive disease extended beyond drugs to negative attitudes about life.

Today I see my value. Sobriety has restored my dignity. I am in touch with the part of me that is noble. In my sobriety, I am a spiritual somebody, not a nobody.

*Let my desire for perfection
be tempered by reality.*

Integrity

"Integrity has no need of rules."
Albert Camus

The benefit of a spiritual program is the development of integrity. Integrity is having an honest respect for myself; it is respecting who I am and how I live.

Integrity is also a bridge by which I reach my fellow and sister humans. Respect for myself nurtures my respect for others. My determination to have integrity affects the way I treat everyone else. Integrity gives me freedom, and this allows for acceptance of others.

I follow rules and guidelines, but today they are not written in cement. I can be flexible. I shed my need to control in favor of serenity and peace. My spiritual program forever teaches me to be free.

*I pray I can see beyond the rules
into the beauty of Integrity.*

Genius

"In the republic of mediocrity, genius is dangerous."
Robert C. Ingersoll

Spirituality is a creative and positive energy that forever seeks new ways to express and improve itself. Spirituality is never satisfied with mediocrity. God is alive in teachers, musicians, writers, singers, and prophets. The standard of excellence is always sought, for the best can always be made better!

As a drunk, I often settled for convenience and mediocrity. My motto was "Why bother? It can be done tomorrow." I had low energy. Addiction robbed me of God's productive energy.

In recovery, I seek the best because I believe I am the best. God made me, and I respect God's choice!

God, save me from the complacence
that makes no demand on my genius.

Hypocrisy

"The devil can cite scripture for his own purpose."
William Shakespeare

Alcoholism is "cunning, baffling, and powerful." I need to walk the talk, make actions fit words, and live my program today rather than talk about it for tomorrow. Why? Because the disease can "talk program" just as fast as I can.

I have caught myself touting things I do not practice. I catch myself admonishing others about principles I do not live by. Today I am aware of my hypocrisy.

I need to recognize this aspect of the disease because I am such a convincing and practiced manipulator! I know I am not perfect, but that should never be an excuse to avoid dealing with my character defects. I must not con myself into staying sick!

Divine Spirit, I pray I may
strive to live the message.

Wine

"One of the disadvantages of wine is that it makes a person mistake words for thoughts."
Samuel Johnson

Alcohol created problems in my life. I was unable to control my drinking, and the result was utter catastrophe. I hurt people. I endangered my health. I ruined my productivity. I became lonely. I felt isolated. I was forever getting into arguments. People who loved me had to walk away from me for their own sanity. Alcohol made my life a mess!

Today I see this, and I am glad I made the spiritual decision to refuse the first drink. I am getting my life together. I am becoming a productive citizen. I have friends and relationships again. But I need to remember what I must never forget:

Alcohol + Me = Problems.

God, alcohol is an offer I can refuse.

Risk

"We should be careful to get out of an experience only the wisdom that is in it."
Mark Twain

I need to risk. I need to try again. I need to face life and not run from it. Early in my sobriety, I was reluctant to try new things because I was afraid I might get hurt. I was afraid to express my feelings. I hid in the idea of simply not drinking. Spirituality is about being willing to reach out into new areas, engage in new and different relationships, and enjoy the richness of God's world.

As I grow in sobriety, I develop the capacity to react differently to painful situations and overcome them. I learn mistakes can make for new conquests. Lasting joys and achievements are born in the risk.

God, teach me to overcome yesterday's sorrows with today's optimism.

Humor

"The one serious conviction one should have is that nothing is to be taken seriously."
Nicholas Murray Butler

I took myself too seriously when I thought everything depended on my thoughts, actions, and decisions. Living was a series of agendas that had to be met. Life was too serious to be joked about. I knew I was not God, but I took responsibility for the whole universe. I had opinions on everything and everybody, and I was always right. As the years passed, my control tactics produced stress, tension, and loneliness.

Then a friend said, "Let go and let God." I began to laugh at myself. I laughed more as I began to accept my humanness. I discovered spirituality in the joke. God must have a sense of humor—after all, God made me!

Help me laugh at myself
in my search for the Kingdom.

July

Belief

"Seek not to understand that you may believe,
but believe that you may understand."
Saint Augustine

I tried to understand my alcoholic behavior only to come away more confused. My efforts to understand sometimes led to dishonesty and manipulation. I drank because I was lonely, angry, or overworked or because I had problems. I tried to understand why. Science has no definitive answer as to why some people are alcoholic other than to postulate the disease factor, with the emphasized advice "Don't pick up the first drink."

Today I do not fully understand why I am an alcoholic. I know I can never drink alcohol without having alcohol problems. My belief keeps me sober and gives me a God I understand and a life I love!

Help me be content with the imperfection
of my knowledge.

Pride

*"There is a paradox in pride: It makes some
ridiculous, but prevents others from becoming so."*
Charles Caleb Colton

Pride can be both creative and negative. I have experienced both in my alcoholic life. When I was drinking, pride made me an arrogant fool. I was unrealistic in
my demands on myself and others, lost in a fantasy of
how I appeared to the outside world. Pride was a mask
behind which I hid my feelings.

In recovery, I am developing love and respect for
myself. I am proud of my achievements and am discovering the "power" God has given me. My program
teaches me to cooperate with God if things are going to
happen in my life. Today I am proud of my willingness
to associate with the God of truth.

*God, let me always treat pride with respect
and be mindful of its destructive attribute.*

Choices

"Destiny is not a matter of chance, it is a matter of choice; it is not a thing to be achieved."
William Jennings Bryan

I create my destiny via the choices I initiate today. In addiction, I was a ship without a sail—drifting through life, tossed in a thousand directions.

Today I point myself in the direction I want to go. This attitude does not take anything away from God's power because God gave me freedom in the first place and gave me the gift of decision making.

God is not a dictator, and I am not a puppet on a string. God loves me enough to allow me to learn from my mistakes and take personal pride in my achievements. Addiction made me powerless. Sobriety puts me in touch with my God-given power.

*Loving Creator, I pray that I might
live responsibly one day at a time.*

Freedom

"Freedom is nothing else but a chance to be better."
Albert Camus

Humans are not puppets. Sometimes, when I hear people talk about God and prayer, the implication is that we have no choice and that all action is determined by God alone. A moment's reflection should make me hesitate about such a viewpoint. Murder, rape, child abuse, and prejudice do not stem from God, but result from the misuse of God's gift of freedom.

As an addict and alcoholic, I know prayers that are not accompanied by actions are mere words. God's love for all people does not obliterate my need to love myself through choice and decision. I experience sobriety and serenity in my life when Divinity is revealed in my choices.

God, help me appreciate my desire to be a winner.

Forgiveness

*"Without forgiveness, life is governed by . . . an
endless cycle of resentment and retaliation."*
Roberto Assagioli

Much of what I resent in others springs from my
unhappiness with myself. I dislike in others what
is negative in me: arrogance, pride, narrow-mindedness,
snobbery, and dishonesty. As long as I refuse to forgive
others, I am not capable of forgiving myself. Part of my
denial is reflected in my attitudes toward others. Those
character traits I refuse to forgive in others are buried
within me.

Today I am learning the difference between forgiveness and acceptance. I can forgive other people without
accepting their lifestyle. I can forgive myself and still see
the need for change. In my forgiveness is the hope for
tomorrow.

*Creator, help me grow in the
forgiveness of self and others.*

Power

"The measure of a person is what he or she does with power."
Pittacus of Mytilene

With my recovery comes a certain success, and with that success comes power. Power comes with the spiritual program, but it must be exercised responsibly. Just as the disease used alcohol to destroy my life, so it can use power to destroy me in sobriety.

Power is a double-edged sword that has led many back to drinking. Certainly, an abuse of power is not consistent with sobriety.

I am respectful of power because I know it can lead to an inflated ego or arrogant personality that continues to destroy the quality of life. I surround myself with friends who will remind me of my roots.

Infinite Spirit, teach me
to exercise power responsibly.

Religion

"Doubt is not the opposite of faith; it is an element of faith."
Paul Tillich

The part of me that does not know is vibrant in spirituality. Problems are part of what it means to be human, and an element of doubt is essential. With doubt comes growth.

When I was younger, I was told it was a sin to doubt. I believed God demanded a steadfast faith in which doubt could have no part! I felt guilty and ashamed about my doubts, but I did have them.

Doubt has always played a part in my life. In some ways, I think my religious doubts have been the most creative part of me. They have certainly enabled me to grow and build a bridge of understanding with others.

God, through my doubts, hear my love for You.

Art

"There is no must in art because it is free."
Vasily Kandinsky

I now understand why throughout history artists were persecuted and why they moved away from organized religion. Many artists search for that which is different, which cannot be contained, and that is spiritually free. As a drinking alcoholic, I found it necessary to control my life, thoughts, and behavior in each and every situation. Sobriety enables me to risk and experiment in God's world.

I am discovering more of myself in what yesterday's artists created. The "musts" of the past have been replaced by the healthy "shoulds" and "needs" of today.

Supreme Artist, let me hear You
in the whisperings of Your creatures.

Pessimism

"There is no sadder sight than a young pessimist."
Mark Twain

I meet many young people who have aged because of their drug addiction. They have lost the spark of youth that is creative and hopeful. Their eyes reveal a powerlessness that keeps them prisoners of lethargy. They do not want to do anything. They walk with no purpose.

Addiction breeds pessimism. Recovery is realizing life need not be like this. True joy and happiness come with the experience of self, rather than chemicals. Reality is facing pain and problems to rediscover the dynamic spirituality of a drug-free existence. Life begins with "No" to drugs. Happiness and confidence are discovered in the "Yes" to life.

Let me see beyond gloom
to the promised sunrise of tomorrow.

Charity

"Must the hunger become anger and anger become fury before anything will be done?"
John Steinbeck

My gratitude stems from the recovery I enjoy. I am happy, joyous, and content. I deal with the daily problems we all face. I am grateful I have a disease from which it is possible to recover. But millions suffer in poverty or with diseases that cannot be arrested by a change in behavior or attitude. What can I do for these people?

I can pray for them. I can visit them or comfort their families when the opportunity arises. But more than this, I can give money to any of the various foundations that require public support. I am aware of my need to give. My gratitude must be grounded in the support of practical charities.

God, let the gratitude I feel enable me to give.

Change

"The foolish and the dead never change their opinion."
James Russell Lowell

My understanding of spirituality tells me I will change my mind, attitude, and opinions. My understanding of sobriety tells me I will grow in understanding of myself, God, and others. I am not afraid to change my thinking.

During my years as an addict, I was fixed and rigid about everything. I saw it as weakness to change my mind. Now I understand I was afraid of change, of not having the answer, of not being in charge.

In treatment, I learned to understand spirituality as reality: seeing things as they are, rather than how I want them to be. I accept that life is about change and that truth is a process toward which I evolve.

In my journey to You, may I have
the willingness to change.

Violence

"Violence is counter-productive and produces changes of a sort you do not want. It is a very dangerous instrument and can destroy those who wield it."

John Gardner

I believed I was not violent when I drank, but that was not true. While I was not physically violent, I used emotional and mental violence. I did not hit, fight, or mutilate people with my hands, but I could tear a person apart with my tongue. My sarcasm and criticism made people cry and feel demoralized and useless. Violence always removes the dignity from people—and I did this with my mouth!

Today I practice tolerance and patience. I count to ten, and when I do lose my temper and hurt a person unfairly or unnecessarily, I apologize. In my sobriety, the anger, hate, and need to hurt are slowly going away. I am progressively getting better a day at a time.

Teacher, let me offer the hand of peace,
not the fist of violence.

Dignity

"To behave with dignity is nothing less than to allow others freely to be themselves."
Sol Chaneles

Ultimately, only I can be responsible for me. It is impossible for me to live another person's life. It is disrespectful to assume the role of decision maker for another adult. People must have the freedom to grow and be themselves. Dignity is affording people this freedom.

Today I see how I continued to keep members of my family sick by taking on responsibilities that were not mine to deal with. I see how I was not treating my family with dignity. I was unintentionally withholding honor from those I loved. People, especially family members, must be given the freedom to express their hurts. They have a responsibility to deal with their pain because it is theirs!

I pray that I may treat others with the dignity I desire in my own life.

Greatness

"The ability to accept responsibility is the measure of the individual."
Roy L. Smith

My greatest insight into life is that I am responsible. My responsibility is an important and dignified gift from God. My responsibility reveals my involvement in God's creation, in my life, and in my recovery from alcoholism.

Greatness is in the choices I make, and my choices come with God's gift of freedom. Human beings are more than puppets on a string or automated machines. We are creative creatures who carry the burden and joy of responsibility.

Along with coming to terms with my alcoholism, I also accepted the responsibility to remain sober in my decisions and lifestyle. Such is greatness.

Thank You for giving me
the responsibility to cocreate.

Music

"I know the twelve notes in each octave and the varieties of rhythm offer me opportunities all of human genius will never exhaust."
Igor Stravinsky

There is so much to be gained in life. Just when I think I have exhausted all possibilities, a new insight is perceived; permutations and variations appear in abundance. One example is sobriety. I thought it meant not drinking, but today I see that it affects all areas of my life: how I walk, the hugs I give, my acceptance of others, my willingness to trust and risk, and my optimism for a new day.

God is comprehensive for me. God is alive in every religion, sacred writing, and tradition. God is also alive in literature, scripture, and music. Today I hear beyond the symphony into the unfathomable message of God's love for all creation.

Thank You for Your messengers who give love through music.

Desire

"One must not lose desires. They are mighty stimulating to creativeness, to love, and to long life."
Alexander A. Bogomoletz

Today I desire to live. I have discovered value in my life. I have experienced personal self-esteem. I am able to feel, talk, trust, and laugh again. I desire to live fully!

I can remember when I felt lonely, isolated, angry, shut down, and hopeless. My desires were destructive when mingled with alcohol. Then the pain became too great and I experienced a vital "moment." I realized I needed to make a choice: Was I to live or die? I chose to live!

This was the beginning of my spiritual journey into self from which I discovered God and this world. Creative and positive desires were reborn in my life, and I am able to live and love again.

God, may I continue to desire
those things that do not hurt me.

Negativity

"My life has been nothing but a failure."
Claude Monet

For years, I considered myself a complete failure. I wallowed on my pity pot until it became too painful. Whatever the payoff was, it had dried up. I was left with a rock-bottom pain that forced me to consider the alternative. Astounding! Impossible! How could this ever be? Was I forever to be a victim of alcoholism? "Not so!" I heard a voice of hope from a recovering alcoholic who had made the change. Slowly, I took steps toward recovery and healing self-esteem.

I am only a failure if I consider myself a failure. I am what I create. God requires my cooperation to make miracles. Listening to those in sobriety provides the seeds for my recovery today.

God, the only real failure is not
seeing You in my life.

Vocation

"It is well for one to respect one's own vocation, whatever it is, and to think oneself bound to uphold it and to claim for it the respect it deserves."
Charles Dickens

Nobody else is quite like me. Nobody else can view, experience, or feel the world the way I can. I am at the center of God's universe. Other people can love, but it is not the same as my love. Other people can offer the hand of friendship, but it is not the same friendship I offer. Other people can utter a kind word, but the phrasing of my words belongs to me.

I am unique and I must remember that. Even my space in the world is special. Nobody can take the place I have on Earth; they cannot get into my space. Others may be looking at the same scene, but I see it from my place in the world. Today I respect my uniqueness.

Let me continue to discover
Your unique image in my life.

Youth

"We are none of us infallible—not even the youngest among us."
W. H. Thompson

When I was younger, I did not want to listen to older people because I felt they did not understand me. Through hindsight, I realize I did not want to hear what they were saying about my lifestyle.

Now that I am a mature adult with some time in sobriety, I must avoid having the same attitude toward the young—that is, not listening to them because I think they are too young or do not understand! I must not repeat, in reverse, yesterday's mistakes!

None of us is infallible. We are not God. We can learn from each other if we have the patience to listen. Often, I need to seek the meaning behind the words.

God, teach me to listen with the ear of understanding and patience.

Worry

"When I look back on all these worries, I remember the story of the old man who said on his deathbed that he had had a lot of trouble in his life, most of which never happened."
Winston Churchill

I can project an incident into a calamity. I can make mountains out of molehills. I can worry myself into the grave.

In the past, I worried about what people meant by what they said. I looked for hidden criticism. I worried about what people were thinking or plotting. If I had nothing to worry about, I then worried because I felt I should have something to worry about!

Today I have a program that helps me deal with this. Of course I still worry, but I have a checklist that keeps me sane and allows me to laugh at the insanity of my projections. Now the worry in my life is not destructive or negative.

Let me bring my worry to You in prayer.

Ignorance

"Not ignorance, but ignorance of ignorance, is the death of knowledge."
Alfred North Whitehead

How little I understood when I was living as an alcoholic. How little I wanted to know. Ignorance was bliss in addiction.

I had no idea how serious my alcoholism was—how it had developed in all areas of my life, how destructive and negative I had become—until I was made to "see" reality in treatment. Reluctantly, I opened my eyes to recognize my ignorance. I knew I needed to change my attitude if I was to recover.

The enemy of the spiritual life is ignorance because it stops me from realizing the strength and healing power of spirituality that has been given by God. All I need do is discover and appreciate it.

I pray for the courage to confront
the ignorance in my life.

Living

"It is not death we should fear, but never beginning to live."
Marcus Aurelius

For years, I did not really live: I simply existed. What many people take for granted I did not have: friends, vacations, job satisfaction, gratitude, family, communication, and love of self. An aspect of my disease was thinking I was happy without any evidence. Indeed, my lifestyle indicated progressive isolation. That is illusion. A recovering alcoholic shared that early in recovery he saw a sunset and remarked, "How long has that been happening?" Like him, I missed so much!

Life can be lived or endured—the choice is mine. My spiritual recovery means every day I reach out to life and grasp it, hold it, smell it—and smile.

God of life, let my living be the glory of the day.

Wealth

"The only question with wealth is what you do with it."

John D. Rockefeller Jr.

Prosperity, if it is truly to be appreciated, needs to be shared. Wealth only makes sense when it is put to use for the benefit of the many. To hoard treasure is to miss its value. Money makes the world go around, but it can only produce joy and excitement when it is spent or put to work.

This is also true for those who have a wealth of ideas or talents, which need to be expressed, shared, and valued by others to be of any real benefit. A writer needs to write, a musician needs to play, a painter demands a canvas—and the world needs to appreciate.

God, too, is at work in this world and requires recognition.

Let me find You in the talents
You have shared with me.

Loneliness

"This great misfortune—to be incapable of solitude."
Jean de la Bruyère

Today I am able to live with loneliness. I know the difference between being alone and being lonely, and even in sobriety I experience loneliness. But today I can live with it. When I was drinking, I had an overwhelming feeling of being lost; now, it is tolerable. I can live with it.

The reality of spirituality demands that I not escape into a fantasy that denies my feelings of loneliness. It is part of my journey toward God. I will never appreciate perfect happiness until I rest in God. This I accept. In sobriety, I have many days of happiness and moments of joy, but I am, at times, lonely. I sometimes have feelings of being lost. Today I can accept this and talk about it.

I accept the part of me that will be
forever lost until I rest in You.

Misfortune

"Experience has taught me this, that we undo ourselves by impatience. Misfortunes have their life and their limits, their sickness and their health."

Michel de Montaigne

Nothing lasts forever. At times I feel sad, angry, resentful, or ashamed—but it passes. In recovery, I have learned to live in my day and accept its consequences. I can only deal with life as I experience it. Some experiences are painful. Reality teaches me this. At times I wish I could go through life without pain or rejection, but I know that is a fantasy. Sobriety does not mean everything will be perfect—only better!

Nothing is so bad that I need to drink or use over it. Today I know alcohol increases my pain; it is never a solution. God, who has given me today, will also give me a tomorrow. Time eases the pain if I work my program. Misfortunes are not worth drinking over.

Thank You for the gift of today.

Adversity

"Adversity reveals genius, prosperity conceals it."
Horace

The only way to understand God, the world, and myself is through some degree of suffering. Pain and suffering are humbling in the truest sense: They stop me from being arrogant, selfish, and prideful. I know this because I was a spoiled child. My family tried to give me everything. It was always my way or no way! That sick love robbed me of humility and separated me from humanity. Being spoiled stopped me from experiencing the real world and stopped me from growing.

Today adversity is part of life and being human. Not to grow through adversity is to die. To feel in life, to have emotion, sometimes entails adversity and pain.

Teach me to be grateful
for the suffering that leads to growth.

Ideas

"Ideas shape the course of history."
John Maynard Keynes

I get excited about sobriety because it has given me
ideas. Today I can think, ponder, and create. God is a
big idea, and everything is involved.

For years, I made God a prisoner of the Church or an
idea in history. In sobriety, I have discovered God in art,
poetry, music, and literature; in friendship, advice, sharing, and sexuality; and in nature, sunsets, animals, and
the sea.

God can be found through my failures. God is perceived in suffering, loneliness, and resentments. The
acknowledgment of my disease has brought me closer to
God as I now understand God. My idea of God is alive
and makes me want to live well.

*May my ideas and thoughts
always reflect Your beauty.*

Similarity

*"Whatever you may be sure of, be sure of this—
that you are dreadfully like other people."*
James Russell Lowell

For many years, I focused on the differences and not the similarities. I was always considering how I was unlike other alcoholics, rather than embracing the striking similarities.

I kept myself on the outside, not only in recovery from alcoholism but also in life. Then I heard from another recovering alcoholic not only "my story" but also my feelings.

I belong. I am with people who know my loneliness, isolation, confusion, guilt, and despair. I have come home to live among my people.

Thank You for showing me I am a member of the human family and a recovering alcoholic.

Playing God

"Greatness is not found in possessions, power, position, or prestige. It is discovered in goodness, humility, service, and character."
William Arthur Ward

How well I remember playing God in my drinking days when, because I had said it, it had to be so! Arrogance and pride kept me lonely and isolated.

My spiritual program teaches me to play God in a healthy way. I must discover the values I associate with God and live them out in my own life. Because I believe God is loving and accepting, I seek to reveal those qualities. It makes no sense to honor a God of truth if I continue to live as a liar.

As a recovering alcoholic, I play God in the joy, acceptance, and love I show myself and other people. I know I am not God! I am God's creation playing along the divine path.

*Let my statements always be open
to the pure light of truth.*

Words

"Hear the meaning within the word."
William Shakespeare

When I hear the word sobriety, I am inspired to think of my relationship with God, others, and, more important, myself. Sobriety means humor, hope, and joy. It means a silence at the center of my being that wonders at it all.

Sobriety means embracing a sexuality that is noble and free, that risks rejection and criticism. Sobriety argues against prejudice and bigotry. It builds a bridge to the different and reflects on the creative variety of humankind. It allows me a God of my understanding but also respects the traditions and ancient philosophies of the world. Sobriety evokes a feeling that is beyond words. It echoes the spiritual life.

Let me learn to pray beyond words.
Let my relationship with You grow in silence.

Temptation

"What makes resisting temptation difficult for many people is that they do not want to discourage it completely."
Franklin P. Jones

Usually I am tempted because I want to be. I allow myself to get too close to the object of my desire, or I invite the problem into my life knowing I will not resist it. Then I use my imperfection as an excuse! In this way, I manipulate my spiritual program and become dishonest.

When I first got sober, I did not allow alcohol in my house. I did not go to bars. I did not spend time with heavy drinkers. I avoided places I associated with alcohol.

This disciplined approach to sobriety worked. If I do not invite the enemy in, I will not get beaten up. I need to remember these simple rules and not become complacent in my abstinence.

Let me keep temptation
out of my life by avoiding it.

August

Self-Reliance

*"The way to greatness is the path of self-reliance,
independence, and steadfastness in times of trial
and stress."*
Herbert Hoover

Today I take responsibility for my life. I take responsibility for my disease. I take responsibility for my
recovery.

I know I am not perfect. While it may be true that I
have many pains and problems yet to face, I take hope in
my daily conquests.

Nothing is too great for me to overcome so long as I
have confidence in myself. It is my "yes" or "no" that
makes the difference. In the power of my choice rests
my freedom.

*God, I thank You for the daily trials
that ensure my victories.*

Laughter

"Nobody ever died of laughter."
Max Beerbohm

I knew I was growing in self-esteem and confidence when I was able to express the belly laugh that proclaims "I am glad to be alive!" Many religious people are too serious. They seem to think God disapproves of laughter, yet laughter is the most natural emotion in the world.

Sobriety is a statement that pain is being overcome, and the hope I experience will necessarily release laughter. Laughter also stops me from treating myself and the world too seriously. Someone once said, "God created the world for fun. Find the key to life and enjoy it." For me, spirituality is that key. Sometimes, my joy is so great I can do nothing but laugh.

Thank You for the gift of laughter.

Understanding

"Humankind—beings in search of meaning."
Plato

I am on my way. Sobriety has brought a desire to understand: life, me, my relationships, and God. My search for meaning includes what is true, what is noble, and what is spiritual.

I no longer wish to hurt, damage, ridicule, destroy, fight, lie, or cheat. I have had enough of being negative; of being lost and isolated in my arrogance; of standing outside life, feeling resentful and afraid. My sobriety involves a search for meaning, knowing full well my understanding will always be imperfect, for I can never comprehend fully. The ultimate answer is in living with confusion. I am not God, but I do intend to reach for the stars.

God, my cry for self-awareness is answered
in the journey, not the destination.

Potential

"Education is helping the child realize his or her potentialities."
Eric Fromm

When I was drinking, I behaved like a child—not childlike but childish. I was so dependent on alcohol that I never realized my potential. I never realized the gift!

Today I have a spiritual program that offers me the world. It sets no limits on my horizons. It encourages me to discover my potential and live it. Now I can learn new languages, visit different countries, enjoy alternative cultures, make new friendships, and, most important, discover the "bigness" of God in this world. The education I have garnered through my sobriety seems unending and unstoppable. Each day produces a new opportunity and a different experience. Every day is a time to receive.

Teach me to journey through the words into the experience.

Thought

"Thought makes the whole dignity of humankind; therefore, endeavor to think well. That is the only morality."

Blaise Pascal

Human beings are very imitative creatures. They imitate clothes, hairstyles, mannerisms, and lifestyles. Their minds are influenced by what they listen to and what they read. As such, what I think is very important to sobriety.

Today I make an effort to examine my thinking and check it out with a sponsor or in a support group. I know my dignity in sobriety is connected not only to what I do but also to my attitudes and thoughts. When my thinking begins to go crazy, I know I am in a dangerous place and I need to talk. God created me with the ability to think; therefore, I need to safeguard the information I put in my mind.

Let me learn to develop morality of mind.

Learning

"If the blind lead the blind, both shall fall into the ditch."
Matthew 15:14

I need to understand before I can teach. I need to listen before I can give advice. I need to associate myself with the winners to become a winner.

For years, I sought advice and direction from many who did not understand. They tried to help but they did not understand. Today I understand part of my denial and manipulation was choosing those who did not understand to help me. This way I could stay sick!

My spiritual journey involves seeking out those who have something I want, and being willing to follow their directions. I surrender to live.

Teach me to develop
a spiritual ego that is teachable.

Prejudice

"There is no more evil thing in the world than race prejudice . . . it justifies and holds together more baseness, cruelty, and abomination than any other sort of error in the world."
H. G. Wells

Something about me fears racism because I fear I may be at risk. If a group of people can be persecuted or ridiculed for being different from others, then why wouldn't it eventually happen to me? With racism, the world is at risk.

Prejudice is the opposite of spirituality. Spirituality always seeks to include, bring together, and unite. The world God has made is ONE. All people and races are a family that must learn to coexist if we are to be productive and creative.

In variety there is strength. With the unusual and peculiar comes Divinity. God is to be found in the confusions of life.

Teacher, give me the courage
to expose the inadequacies in my life.

Money

"Money often costs too much."
Ralph Waldo Emerson

Money can be a curse. It can destroy people. Money in itself has no value. It needs to be used and put to work. Many people think it can work miracles: make them happy, give them self-esteem, bring love into their lives, remove their loneliness, cure their insecurities, and remove their alcohol or drug problems! The historical list of wealthy casualties indicates this is not the case.

Because I have a compulsive nature, I need to be aware of my desire for money and the responsible way I need to use it. Spirituality involves the use of money. I need to be positive in my attitude toward money and creative in my use of it.

*O God, may I allow money to serve me and
never be foolish enough to serve it.*

Acceptance

"One who has become a thinking being feels a compulsion to give to every creature the same reverence for life one gives one's own."
Albert Schweitzer

Today I accept people. Even the people with whom I do not agree, I accept. My freedom is dependent upon my attitude toward others. My respect is rooted in the respect I give others. Nowhere is this more true for me as a spiritual person than in my attitude toward people of other creeds—and those who have none! The spiritual life that unites me to God and the world requires my acceptance of difference and recognition of my personal need for it. Even those who hurt, abuse, or destroy must be accepted from within because something of their life exists in mine. In this accepting love lies the daily healing of my disease.

May my acceptance of the tyrant
lead to my forgiveness of self.

Faith

"Faith must trample underfoot all reason, sense, and understanding."
Martin Luther

An obstacle to understanding the spiritual life was my intellectualization. My head was forever getting in the way of my heart. It was much easier for me to think than feel. My faith was smothered by logic. My mind kept me from experiencing the adventure of faith.

The poet in me has grown as I have begun to trust others. God becomes alive in my confusion. The answer is in not having all the answers. Spirituality involves all the varied confusions and paradoxes of life I have discovered in me and in others, and that is okay. Today the love I give and receive is beyond my wildest dreams. I smile at the joy of my confusion.

May my head unite with
my heart in the daily maze of life.

Individuality

"Treat people as if they were what they ought to be, and you help them become what they are capable of being."
Johann Wolfgang von Goethe

My spiritual program involves a love of self. This inspires me to get in touch with my individuality. Although I can identify with other people's feelings and situations, we are also not exactly the same. Our dreams and aspirations are different, our gifts and achievements vary, and our individuality adds to the variety.

My difference needs to be nurtured alongside my spiritual growth. This is especially true because as a recovering alcoholic I am tempted to "please" the crowd. Today my personal inventory revolves around my needs, hopes, and dreams that are realistic. Spirituality is reality.

Thank You for making the world with such creative difference.

Life

"The tragedy of life is what dies in us while we live."
Albert Schweitzer

Addiction progressively takes away the vitality of life. It robs us of meaning. Addiction isolates; it kills by atrophy: People, places, and things lose meaning and God is lost.

To compensate, I used to say I was having fun. I said this a lot and at times believed it, but in the silence of the night I knew it was a lie. I lied to others and myself. At that point, I would have begun to die had I not had the courage to face the truth.

Today I live because I confronted my lie. I discovered the spiritual power buried deep beneath the progressive addiction. Now I find it easier to live.

May I continue to breathe a daily "yes" in my life that I might continue to live in Your truth.

Reality

"Humankind cannot bear very much reality."
T. S. Eliot

I wonder why I sometimes find it hard to face reality? In the past, I preferred to escape from my problems, avoid who I was, and not deal with issues of God, relationships, or loneliness. Essentially, I lived in a world of make-believe. However, it did not work. The pain of being a fake and living a lie became too great. Eventually, I asked for help.

Today I am on a journey to reality, and it is a spiritual pilgrimage. I know I will never be completely real. A part of me will always be diseased. I must live and treat my compulsive behavior on a daily basis, but my life is getting better. I am slowly growing in my understanding of who I am and what I need.

God, let me be as real as I can be.

Truth

"If error is corrected whenever it is recognized as such, the path of error is the path of truth."
Hans Reichenbach

I believe that to discover spirituality in my life, I need to confront the disease—that destructive and negative side of myself. I need to make the disease work for me! For many years, I tried to avoid and deny my alcoholism. I wanted to recover by osmosis! I did not want to get my hands dirty with the reality of suffering. Instead, I expected a miracle to make everything different.

I did not want to face my pain! But it does not work that way. If I am to get well, I need to confront my disease, smell my disease, hold my disease, pull and tug at the disease in my life. I can make my disease work for me; that is spirituality.

Let me have the courage to pass through the pain and experience the gain.

Property

"Property is the fruit of labor. Property is desirable; it is a positive good."
Abraham Lincoln

God is manifest everywhere, including the physical. God is found in my body, in my sexuality, in mountains and streams, and in houses and real estate. The luxury and comfort of good living are not incompatible with the spiritual life. Indeed, the use of property can be an opportunity for gratitude and sharing.

I know many people who use their comfortable homes for opportunities to develop sincere friendships. Property is part of God's landscape in the world. God's love, joy, and hope for humankind can be experienced by my creative use of property.

Let me use my property creatively
and for the good.

Sacrifice

"To believe in sensible ideas is easy, but to implement them involves sacrifice."
Dorothy Fosdick

What am I prepared to sacrifice for what I want? I remember the time I said I would do anything.

Today I know "anything" must be translated into something. No person, job, or thing can be allowed to come between me and my abstinence. This love of self will enable me to love others. But I must remember to examine my desire to please others and be willing to hold my own needs as a priority in my life.

I know if I do not love myself enough to make sacrifices, I can be nothing. In gratitude, I give up those things I know will hurt me and embrace those things I know will support me.

Everlasting Spirit, may I choose wisely that which I sacrifice and that which I keep.

Courage

"Nothing will ever be attempted if all possible objections must be first overcome."
Samuel Johnson

There was a time I never attempted anything because I said it could not be done. I believed I could never get sober. I feared I could never stand up to my drunken friends. I knew I could never face my buried secrets.

Then I saw confidence and hope reflected in people who were recovering from these same problems. I heard people talk about what it was like, what happened, and what it is like now. They told me that by saying "I can't" I really meant "I won't!"

The same people encouraged me to take a risk, to think positive, to go ahead and try. Today yesterday's objections are mere memories.

Thank You for showing me the light at the end of the tunnel. May I continue to walk in grace.

Ability

"Our ability is derived from God and does not have to be acquired."
James H. McReynolds

I awoke this morning and remembered that sobriety and serenity are gifts from God that are freely given. I need only discover these gifts within my own capacity to be honest. I need only seek them in my new attitudes. I need only discover them in the spiritual program from my life.

My ability can only be limited by my fear of success. Today I have a strong program that encourages me to succeed. I am surrounded by others in recovery who support me to share my gifts with the world.

In courage, I move forward. God is alive in my life, and God's acceptance of me is guaranteed.

*May I continue to discover
more of Your beauty in my life.*

Decision

"When you see a snake, never mind where it came from."
W. G. Benham

M any alcoholics have died looking for the "problem" that made them drink. They needed to pinpoint their spouse, family, community, church, or job as the reason they got drunk. They died seeking an excuse. Alcoholics Anonymous clearly states that alcohol is the problem for alcoholics. Alcohol is the problem! This statement is simple, yet profound in its healing implications.

Today thousands are choosing not to die by not taking the first drink. To see the problem clearly and honestly is the beginning of wisdom. My recovery is in my own hands; my addiction is my responsibility. There is no one or nothing else to blame.

Teach me to avoid those things
that cause me pain and destruction.

Togetherness

"One who thinks of oneself as belonging to a particular national group in America has not yet become an American."
Woodrow Wilson

Today I know I belong. I am not alone. I do not exist outside the human race. I am an important part of this world.

Addiction made me feel different, separate, and isolated. It kept me divided within my family, my relationships, and myself. As long as I allowed it to do this, addiction was winning. Now I know I belong. I am a part of the whole. Something of this universe is mine. I am not an island unto myself. I am an essential part of the human race. I am at home in my world.

Eternal Giver, I cherish the gift of unity.

Happiness

"We are looking in the wrong places for happiness."
Robert J. McCracken

I sought happiness in the bottle. Others looked for good feelings in drugs, food, gambling, sex, spending, or other people.

Today I know nothing outside me can make me acceptable; acceptance must come from within. I need to discover the spiritual place in which I can be acceptable to me. Self-esteem is an essential part of my recovery and can only be realized by making the spiritual journey within.

Sobriety allows me to see more clearly. My program gives me tools to do the work. Healthy friends support and care about me. Happiness is my responsibility. It is always within my reach; all I have to do is look in the right place.

I seek to discover happiness. I want to know myself because You created me.

Indifference

*"The worst sin toward our fellow and sister crea-
tures is not to hate them, but to be indifferent to
them. That is the essence of inhumanity."*
George Bernard Shaw

For years, I was indifferent to family and friends. The
real tragedy was that because of my alcoholism, I did
not know I treated others this way! I was unaware of my
disease and its implications.

Today I am not indifferent. Spirituality teaches me
that I am not a spectator but a participant. I am involved
in my life and the lives of others. I practice the principles
of sobriety in every area of my life. I seek not only to be
sober on a daily basis but also to be honest, open, and
tolerant.

The spiritual goal of sobriety and abstinence has
placed me at the center of the universe. I know I make a
difference to my fellow and sister humans.

*Remove from me all attitudes of indifference
and apathy. Make me a worthy steward
of Your love.*

Confidence

"There is no sort of work that could ever be done well if you minded what fools say."
George Eliot

Part of the risk in recovery is arousing the displeasure of others. I know I cannot please all the people all the time, yet my disease tells me I must! For years, I missed opportunities because I listened to negative and frightened people. Now, I shout my "Yes!" to life and ignore the fools. Those fools are rarely friends. Rather, they seek to keep me in the same prison in which they trap themselves. If they truly loved me, they would encourage me to be imaginative and creative.

Today I take a joyride by "letting go and letting God" because God is a great risk taker! When I tap into God's wisdom, I live my life with confidence.

May I embrace the advice of others but never
squander my own power of decision.

Limitations

"Why would we kill off a good watchdog just because he could not fly?"
Frank Mar

God created the world with variety, and we all have different gifts. Some people make music, others write stories, and many are practical in industry or the home. I need to understand the gifts and skills I have and develop those. It is fruitless to spend my time complaining I am not like other people, that I am not blessed with their talents. Such an attitude stops me from discovering my own creative talents. By comparing myself with others, I miss my own uniqueness.

Today I enjoy discovering more about myself and the abundant gifts God has freely given me. This healthy outlook allows me to recognize others' gifts while celebrating my own.

I pray that I may be truly grateful
for what I have.

Temper

"Your temper is the only thing that does not get better with age."
Anonymous

When I was active in my addiction, I lost my temper anytime I feared I was in the wrong and needed to protect myself. My temper was closely associated with my ego and pride. I hated to admit I was in error.

Today I know I am not God. I sometimes make mistakes. When this happens, I apologize. I do not always have to have the answer. It is okay to be imperfect and human.

As I grow in self-acceptance, I am no longer invested in being right, and my fear naturally subsides. By following the steps to recovery, I find I do not lose my temper so much!

May I express my anger or discomfort
in constructive and effective ways.

Security

"Nobody in this world is more secure than a person in a penitentiary."
Harvey S. Firestone Jr.

I n one sense, it is safe to live in a prison—but at what price? To live is to be free, and to be free is to have the responsibility of choice. Addiction obliterates my power of choice and takes away my freedom.

In sobriety, I am involved in the joys of risking. I experience the pleasure and pain that come with the responsibility of choice. My recovery brings a new and healthier sense of security. I welcome challenges because I know I am free to choose.

Now the prison of addiction is not my reality. Today I know I am living; yesterday, I had to read about it!

God, I thank you for the confusing gift of freedom.

Purpose

"I have never doubted that God created us for great purposes."
Preston Bradley

I am special. I know there is a purpose for my life. That purpose is essentially good and creative. I realize beauty is not only in the things I can see; beauty is also in the unseen, which includes my innermost self.

Today I affirm my great purpose in this world: to be the best I can be! My recovery allows me to live this dream.

For too many years, I gave my God-ordained power away to alcohol, people, and a belief system that did not make sense. Now I am discovering the power God has bestowed upon me, and I feel good about myself. I reclaim my Divinity right here and right now.

Creator of this wonderful universe,
make me an instrument of Your peace.

Character

"One never discloses one's own character so clearly as when one describes another's."
Johann Paul Richter

I was always perceptive when it came to assessing the character faults of others. I could offer the best advice in the world. I was excellent at "pulling the covers" on a con artist, but somehow I missed me! I never really heard the insights I shared. I never followed my own advice. I always minimized my own character faults. Usually, what I saw in others was reflected in my own personality. The things I loathed in others existed in me. The anger and resentment came from a denial of self.

In sobriety, I hear the advice of others. I do not always like it, but I hear it. I share healthy criticism when asked and am growing in my acceptance of others' healthy criticism of me.

In others, may I see clearly my own reflection.

Education

"The university exists only to find and communi-cate the truth."
Robert Maynard Hutchins

In recovery, I am a student of Truth. No longer do I search for a cheap thrill or quick fix. Now I desire last-ing truth.

Spirituality is finding God in things that are true and honest, good and wholesome, and creative and positive. I still battle with the side of me that is greedy, selfish, and dishonest. I am not perfect. I know my former sick and dishonest way of living does not work. My history has taught me that. I was never happy knowing my gains came at the expense of others.

I am a student in the University of Life! I enjoy learn-ing something new about myself every day. Today I listen to those who are wiser than I.

God, who lives in and through Truth,
continue to illuminate my life.

Listening

"If other people are not going to talk, conversation becomes impossible."
James McNeill Whistler

In my addiction, I never listened to what people were saying, owing to my arrogance, denial, fear, control, and ego. I was bored and unhappy because I was a prisoner of my own thoughts.

My spiritual awakening—which is a process rather than an event and ever unfolding—allowed new information into my realm of understanding that led to admittance and acceptance. The day I was able to admit I was an alcoholic was the day I took a step toward wellness. Today I receive immense help and comfort from others, especially recovering alcoholics. Two or more people experiencing an honest conversation are part of God's promised love for this world.

May I honor Your divine message
in the words of others.

Style

"Style is the person himself or herself."
Georges-Louis Leclerc

Style is part of spirituality, especially when it concerns the recovering addict. Sobriety and serenity are seen not only in what I say or do or in my ability to keep away from the first drink or pill but also in my creative style. How I feel about myself should be seen in the confidence of my gait and my concern with a pleasing appearance. Personal hygiene reflects my love of self. Healthy habits and physical exercise reveal my desire for and interest in life, fitness, wellness, and energy.

Well-being is part of the divine birthright I am discovering in recovery. Style may not make the person, but it certainly reveals the individual. Today I want to show the best of myself—inside and out!

May I reveal Your beauty
in my own appearance and style.

September

Optimism

"Optimism is a kind of heart stimulant—the digitalis of failure."
Elbert Hubbard

Today I am an optimist. I believe in life and, more important, I believe in me. I know God cares, and this brings me hope.

When I was drinking, I had a negative and destructive attitude in all areas of my life. Back then, nothing pleased me, people were not to be trusted, everybody had a price, God seemed to be out to lunch, and life had lost its meaning. I was a sad, lonely, and angry individual.

When I was told to put down the drink and follow some new directions, I agreed halfheartedly. I met people who laughed, shared their pain, and lived in the realistic now. I began to listen. Slowly, I changed. Now peace is within my grasp.

Teach me to look beyond the shadows
to the light of Your radiance.

Memory

*"Every person's memory is his or her private
literature."*
Aldous Huxley

What it was like. What happened. What it is like
now. Memory. If I am to stay sober, I need to
remember on a daily basis. I must never forget. Life is
reflected in memory. The writing on the wall is really in
my head, but am I prepared to acknowledge it? For years,
I chose not to remember. Through denial, I would forget and drink again, only to awaken to yesterday's pain
once more.

Memory is a key to my recovery. Spirituality is seeing
my life as it is, rather than how I imagined or hoped it
would be. My pain belongs in my life because it is mine!
Does alcohol work for or against me? Remembering
helps me answer that question today and hopefully
tomorrow.

*Thank You, God, for allowing
my yesterdays to forge my tomorrows.*

Solitude

"One of the greatest necessities in America is to discover creative solitude."
Carl Sandburg

Every now and then, and sometimes more often than others, I need to be alone. Being alone is not the same as being lonely. I need to be alone with me to love and understand myself, hear my needs, and plan my day.

Solitude is a spiritual experience because it enables me to center on what God is doing and creating in my life. Solitude allows me to think and cooperate with God's will for me in the world.

As a practicing addict, I was always running around being busy. Today I rest within myself to be more active and creative.

Let me be still so that I can enjoy my world.

Humility

"Humility is to make a right estimate of one's self."
Charles Haddon Spurgeon

To see myself as a good person is part of the program of humility. To see my gifts and recognize my achievements is what it is to be a humble person. God does not make junk; therefore, I should not act or behave toward myself in a way that indicates anything besides how special I am.

As an addict and alcoholic, I need to accept this, because for years I felt guilty, lonely, and ashamed. These attitudes helped keep me sick.

Sobriety and serenity are recognizing the God-given uniqueness that makes me special. I can achieve great things as long as I continue to believe in myself.

Thank You for allowing me to be a part of You.

Nature

"All are but parts of one stupendous whole, whose body nature is and God the soul."
Alexander Pope

I belong to this mighty universe, but more important, it belongs to me. I have a responsibility in and to the world. No longer can I abrogate that responsibility.

God created me and is creating through my life now. Sobriety allows me to feel this oneness. I stand on a mountaintop, look at the rolling hills beyond, and feel noble. Birds sing, streams murmur, and I feel a tremendous sense of joy. I also feel the pain of the world. People suffering, pointless violence, and the injustice of prejudice—all this I feel, too. Spirituality involves intermixture and allows for paradox. Today I recognize my place in the scheme of things and consciously do my part.

Thank You for including me in
Your design for life.
I tremble at the responsibility.

Fear

"The only thing we have to fear is fear itself."
Franklin Delano Roosevelt

Fear is a killer. It is a killer because it drains me of life, energy, and creativity. Fear petrifies the human spirit.

I spent a lot of yesterdays in fear of people finding out, of the telephone ringing, of where it would all end. I was afraid of me! I did not realize I was feeding the fear with my own behavior. I drank myself into fear. The day I stopped drinking alcohol was the day I stopped giving energy to my fear.

Today I live my life free of abnormal or unrealistic fears. I enjoy my life. I work through my problems. I am not afraid of my shadow. Today I love me.

May I always connect my unrealistic fears with my behavior—and begin the process of change.

Work

"Without work all life goes rotten."
Albert Camus

Work opens the door to the meaning of life and stops my experience from being boring and dull. Work is creative. When I was drinking, I could not reap the benefit of this understanding. As such, work became a burden, something I had to get through, and something I had to do for money and security. I missed the creative dynamic of work and how it could empower me to feel good about myself.

In recovery, I work, create, and grow not only in my job but also in my leisure hours. Today the program I take into the office is the same program I take into places of recreation or repose. God is everywhere and in everything.

Dear God, in the many aspects
of my work, may I feel alive.

Lies

"A liar needs a good memory."
Quintilian

In the past, I lied to impress, to hide my guilt and shame, to cover my mistakes, to bridge silence, and to give life to my fantasies. I lied to hurt and destroy.

As time went by, I lied to cover the lies. Then I lied to cover the lies I told to cover the original lies! And so it went: endless, exhausting, and meaningless. A part of me always loathed the lies I told. Then I grew to hate myself.

Today because I understand spirituality is based on truth, I try not to tell lies. If and when I do lie, I make an effort to correct myself and apologize. In recovery, lying is painful for me. Now I try to use my mind, imagination, and memory for better things.

God, who gave the miracle of communication, may I not abuse Your gift by deceit.

Religion

"Science without religion is lame; religion without science is blind."

Albert Einstein

In recovery, I need to work with others and listen to the professionalism we all bring. The answer is often found among the many. Too often, I segregated myself in a ghetto of learning and missed what others were saying—and the disease won! That behavior reminds me of the old days in the Church when science was seen as the enemy. Pride and ego kept people sick, isolated, and afraid, and thousands suffered and died as a result.

Now people have begun to listen to each other and the world benefits from shared wisdom. Growth occurs via spirituality, which always reaches beyond the bounds of any religion. We need to listen to each other—and listening begins with me!

May I recognize You in the honest experience of every person.

Neighbors

"The good neighbor looks beyond the external accidents and discerns those inner qualities that make all of us human and, therefore, brothers and sisters."
Martin Luther King Jr.

As a drunk, I said cruel things. My prejudice hid my insecurity. I condemned in others what I did not like in myself. I deflected negative attention by calling others names. This was sick manipulation. Neighbor was only a word I could spell or interpret in the service of pretentious innuendo; it was not a concept I truly understood or experienced.

Today I am a good neighbor to many people, known and unknown. Recovery has brought new faces to my life. Relationships mean something. Friends are important. I see the world as one.

In the stranger I discover something of myself. The foreigner has become both friend and neighbor.

I never cease to be amazed at Your mystery and variety, which is manifest in me and all others.

Thought

"To be able to be caught up in a world of thought—that is being educated."
Edith Hamilton

For years, I did not actually think; I simply reacted. Things happened and I felt I had to respond, but rarely was my response carefully considered.

Today I think before I speak. I talk things over with a sponsor or friends before making important decisions. I listen to the opinions of others before choosing. I am caught up in a world of thought that is not simply my own. God knows my best thinking nearly killed me!

The world only makes sense when people share. Giving and receiving make life worthwhile. To be an island unto myself is isolation. I know what it is to be lonely. Today I desire a relationship of mind, body, and feelings.

Let me find You in my neighbor
and be prospered by the stranger.

Self-Love

"To love oneself is the beginning of a lifelong romance."
Oscar Wilde

Today I love myself. To love myself is to love God and the world. I cannot befriend others without first having a relationship with myself. I am the most important part of my existence. I do not say this in conceit but in the spirit of self-love. This truth reveals healthy pride and respect for my life—and it feels good!

For years, I thought love of "self" was wrong and sinful, a misuse of energy and time. What people thought or said about me was a constant worry. The more I looked outside myself for meaning, the more isolated and confused I became. Then I heard God loved me and wanted me to love me. Today I live and love through me.

God, who created me to love,
let love begin with me.

Minority

*"The greatest good of a minority of our
generation may be the greatest good for the
greatest number of people in the long run."*
Oliver Wendell Holmes Jr.

I belong to a minority. I am a recovering alcoholic. I
have a spiritual program that keeps me sober one day
at a time. I have a God I can understand. I take a daily
inventory and make amends when appropriate—and I
feel good about myself.

This spiritual program is reaching out to the world:
gamblers, overeaters, cocaine addicts, the families of
addicts, and the children of compulsive people. Obsessive people of any sort can all be helped by this daily program of acceptance. Perhaps the recovering drunk has
stumbled upon a miracle that can bring the world back
to God! Today I do my part by staying clean and sober,
and I rejoice in the recovering minority to which I
belong.

*God, the more I talk about my difference
with people, the more I feel the same.*

Middle Age

"Middle age is when you begin to smile at things that used to cause you to laugh."
Anonymous

Today I feel so young at heart. I love to laugh—really laugh. I love to have fun and act silly in my life. I love discovering the inner child who comes out to play and gives balance to my life.

This was not always the case. Not too many yesterdays ago, I was serious and depressed, affecting a smile that did not come from within. Alcoholism made me an unhappy person. Before I got sober, my so-called "high" had changed into a boring low!

Back then, I was middle-aged way before my time. Today regardless of my age, I feel younger than ever—and it shows. I am what I drink. Today I am sober!

Ageless Spirit, may I be created anew each day.

Nonsense

"We find it hard to believe other people's thoughts are as silly as our own, but they probably are."
James Harvey Robinson

Today I am able to laugh at myself. I even think funny things. As I sit in a park, restaurant, or airport, I observe the faces, postures, and mannerisms of the people passing by, and I smile, giggle, and laugh to myself in a joyful way. Then I think about what a funny individual I am—sometimes ridiculously proud, sometimes pompous about the silliest things, sometimes preoccupied about my own importance—and I laugh even louder.

Yes, today I am able to laugh at myself. I know people are funny because I know I am. I appreciate myself as a work in progress. Recovery allows me to lighten up. After all, God must have a sense of humor to have made me!

Thank You for the gift of humor
that allows my true humility to develop.

Denial

"The worst vice of the fanatic is sincerity."
Oscar Wilde

Alcoholism is "cunning, baffling, and powerful." It manipulated me to believe the lie. I reached a point in my disease when I believed my crazy behavior was acceptable. Insanity was the order of the day. When friends or therapists tried to give me a message, I discounted them.

To break down the wall of denial, I must recognize strength in numbers. When everybody I respect disagrees with me, it is time for me to change. If my isolation has become a source of martyrdom, I need to reorganize my attitude toward living. I need always stay close to my recovering community. Strength and sobriety are found in numbers. I allow others to support me on the path out of denial.

God, help me live Your truth
in my recovering community.

People-Pleasing

"I cannot give you the formula for success, but I can give you the formula for failure, which is try to please everybody."
Herbert Bayard Swope

Recovery does not demand that I never people-please, but it does ask that I recognize when I am doing it. My low self-esteem was revealed in the way I said and did what others wanted. All that time, I missed life because I was preoccupied with other people. I was never honest. I hated being that way, but I refused to admit it. Now I see how the guilt led me into that sick cycle. Recovery is taking me out of it.

Today, when appropriate, I do not hesitate to say "I don't agree with you." When the occasion calls for it, I am not afraid to confidently state "I refuse to do that." I am discovering the dignity of my straightforwardness.

Great Spirit, may I have the courage
to share my true feelings.

Open-Mindedness

"A fanatic is one who cannot change one's mind and will not change the subject."
Winston Churchill

I had a closed mind because I was afraid to be wrong. I had to be right, in control, and perfect. To say "I don't know the answer" would have made me weak, vulnerable, and downright human! As time passed, I developed mental isolation via my thoughts, my ideas, my life, and my God. Through it all, I was in pain.

Then I experienced a moment of clarity. I realized I was sick and if I really wanted help I could receive it. I put away the alcohol and became vulnerable. I faced life and discovered I was not alone. Spirituality is more about living with the questions than providing the answers. By being open-minded, I ensure my continued growth.

May I continue to be open to Your truth.

Suicide

"Often the test of courage is not to die but to live."
Count Vittorio Alfieri

There are many ways of committing suicide. The obvious way is to take one's own life—the ultimate escape. One can reach the point where there seems to be no hope, no purpose in living, and death may appear attractive. Many alcoholics and addicts reach this level of despair.

There is a more subtle method of suicide, which is to kill oneself slowly by practicing sick behavior and a negative attitude. I was dying in a lifestyle that revolved around alcohol. All I wanted to do was drink. I was dying in my own life, committing suicide by degree!

Today I see this and am grateful I had the courage to live. My act of courage began with my "No" to alcohol.

Let me continue to live in my life.

Sharing

"The mass of humankind leads lives of quiet desperation."
Henry David Thoreau

I thought I was the only one who felt like I did. Nobody could possibly understand. I was different and needed to keep my life secret. I was living in quiet desperation! Then I went to a meeting for recovering alcoholics and heard somebody share my pain, loneliness, confusion, and addiction—my life. I realized I was lonely because I kept myself separate. I saw them as different, so I remained the lonely and isolated victim.

Strange how similar we are when we begin to share. When I see beyond culture, class, and creed, I discover sensitive human beings trying to make sense of their lives. We need each other. I need others.

May I risk reflection in my spiritual
need to share and be known.

Action

"I shall pass through this world but once. If, therefore, there be any kindness I can show, or any good thing I can do, let me do it now; let me not defer it or neglect it, for I shall not pass this way again."
Etienne de Grellet

God requires me to be involved in my recovery and sobriety. God has always wanted me to be sober, but the miracle took place when I also wanted it. God's hand was always extended to me, but the miracle happened when I chose to embrace God. Now I understand sobriety is much more than simply "not picking up the first drink." Recovery involves quiet acts of kindness to myself and others.

God works through my hands, smile, voice, love, and acceptance. When an opportunity arises for me to be kind, I intend to answer the call. I often needed such kindness in the past and rejoice in giving the gift to others who need it now.

*May I never avoid an opportunity
for shared healing.*

Heaven

"If you're not allowed to laugh in heaven, I don't want to go there."
Martin Luther

As a practicing alcoholic, I imagined heaven to be a dull, formal place, rather like a never-ending cathedral—beautiful but serious. My pain and guilt were so great I rarely laughed. When I did, it was often inappropriate and violent—I usually only laughed at others!

Today my heaven is associated with recovery. It is a place of joy, acceptance, and forgiveness. It is a place people can be themselves, an environment in which variety abounds. The laughter of peace resonates.

Heaven is not unlike the places I have discovered in sobriety. I am at one with my Creator and all my brothers and sisters. I am home!

God of Love, when I hear laughter here on Earth, I feel I am in heaven.

Love

"Take away love and our Earth is a tomb."
Robert Browning

Spirituality is essentially love. It is the love that suffers and grows in the acceptance of my compulsive and obsessive behavior. It is the love that requires knowledge of self to give understanding and respect to others.

Spirituality is the loving vulnerability that creates healing in my recovery. It provides meaning in my life and relationships.

The world is a creative place, and I will only find happiness when I begin to create. God created me to take and make, give and receive. With the suffering, loneliness, struggle, and acceptance comes a love that is real and alive.

Teach me to live my life and not merely exist.

God

"God is not a cosmic bellboy."
Harry Emerson Fosdick

My understanding of God unfolds within the context of freedom. God is involved in the world but allows me autonomy. I am not a puppet on a string. When things begin to go wrong, God does not interfere or make changes without my cooperation. God reveals love by allowing me creative responsibility.

For years, I did not understand this. I thought if I prayed enough, God would answer and come to my rescue. When that did not happen, I grew confused, angry, and resentful. What was I doing wrong? Where was God in my life?

Today I appreciate God's detachment. I grow in freedom. I cooperate with God's miracle.

*God, thank You for allowing me
the freedom to fail.*

Prayer

"Prayer is not asking. It is a language of the soul."
Mohandas K. Gandhi

As a child, I was told prayer is "talking to God." Later, I discovered prayer is more than this: Prayer is a relationship with God. It is a two-way system in which I talk to God but must also listen.

Like any relationship that is going to work and grow, this needs time. I must spend time developing my relationship with God. I must create an awareness of this presence in my life because I believe God is always there for me.

But more than this, prayer is a yearning for truth at the center of my being. In prayer I get in touch with the part of me that will be forever restless until I truly find God.

Dear God, prayer is my journey to You.

Pain

"You cannot hold someone down without staying down with them."
Booker T. Washington

I know who was holding me down in my life—I was. I know who was bringing pain and sadness to my life—I was. I know who was making me the victim of addiction—I was.

I would beat myself up, then complain about the bruises! I did this because I could not see. I had not yet understood or accepted the implications of my alcoholism.

Today I am beginning to take care of myself and have accepted my disease. I no longer choose to be the enemy in my life. I have surrendered to the process. I do not want to hurt anymore. I do not want to hide in guilt or fear. I do not choose to be my own victim today.

*God, thank You for the freedom
to determine my life and my victories.*

Achievement

"Do not mistake activity for achievement."
Mabel Newcomber

I sometimes run in circles and get nowhere. I spend forever doing things, yet I know I am not achieving anything. At times, it seems I am going nowhere!

"Be still and know that I am God." I need to stop. I need to listen to the pain within. I need to relax in my gratitude. I need to rest in myself. I do not have to achieve everything all at once, and I do not have to work alone. Recovery has taught me to take life one day at a time. I am comfortable going with the flow. I can be proactive while trusting the process.

I no longer worry I will miss something if I do not control every moment. Tomorrow has not yet come. Today I take time for me.

God, I hear Your still small voice, and I listen.

Mistakes

"Good people are good because they have come to wisdom through failure."
William Saroyan

Today I learn from my mistakes because I understand they really were mistakes! My biggest mistake was trying to drink alcohol like a nonalcoholic.

Drugs do not think; they react. They always work, and they worked against me. Most of my failures stemmed from my misconception of a basic fact: Alcoholics cannot drink like nonalcoholics! This I now accept. I am stronger for having lived through my alcoholism. God is more real, the world more comprehensible, and my life more understandable because of the pain.

If a part of goodness is knowing I am not perfect, then on a daily basis I am becoming a good person.

God, who made a world that includes mistakes, help me accept mine as a vehicle to wisdom.

Blackouts

"It is human nature to think wisely and act foolishly."
Anatole France

I experienced blackouts in my drinking. Often, I woke up not knowing where I had been, or what I had said or done. I would rise to peer through windows searching for my car. I would telephone to find out what time I had left the party and whether anything had happened.

There were other times I knew what I had done, knew what I had said, and remembered how I had behaved, and yet went back for more. I drank "alcoholically" for years because my pride would not allow me to be alcoholic. I created the wisest excuses for staying sick!

Today my sobriety requires a wisdom that is based in reality. From this center, I grow in the light one day at a time.

God of action, teach me to align
my feet with my best thinking.

Patience

*"Prayer of the modern American: 'Dear God, I
pray for patience. And I want it right now!'"*
Oren Arnold

I appreciate those times when I experience the gift of
patience in my life, though it does not happen as often
as I would like. That is an interesting point: I am impa-
tient about having patience!

True patience sometimes requires me to back off and
allow God into the driver's seat, resting in the knowledge that things happen in divine time. This does not
mean I am not involved, but it allows for God's comprehensive plan to unfold.

I often experience patience when I get in touch with
gratitude. Once I stop giving energy to the "I wants," the
joy of serenity breathes through my life and I can relax.
Sometimes I simply need to stop and say "Thank you."

*God, let me breathe these words
into my life: "Thy will be done."*

Laughter

"We are all here for a spell; get all the good laughs you can."
Will Rogers

When I first heard recovering alcoholics laughing, I thought I was in the wrong place. I was angry that they treated the disease so lightly. Then I began to see how laughter is part of a deep joy that comes with healing. It is a spiritual, positive response to life—the noise of optimism.

There is so much in life for me to laugh about, not only the funny things I did but also the humor that abounds in living. How funny is my self-righteousness? How amusing am I in courtship? How ridiculous do I appear when I pretend to be serious and in charge?

I am ready to laugh at myself and grow in the process. Laughter is the conversation of angels.

Let me see the miracle of humor
in the gift of life and be prepared to share it.

Reality

"The books the world calls immoral are the books that show the world its own shame."
Oscar Wilde

In my addiction, I avoided things I did not like or did not want to consider. I hid from life and condemned things I did not wish to understand. My ego created a hypocritical purity that caused me to judge, condemn, and abuse the thoughts and ideas of those I considered inferior.

Today I live and let live—not to avoid conflict or criticism but because I have found, through experience, how my ideas and attitudes have changed during my years of recovery. People I would have condemned to hell are now my friends and mentors. Concepts and lifestyles that were once abhorrent to me are now appreciated and inspiring. What was once dismissed as immoral is part of my life.

God of truth and reality, help me
accept the difference in others.

Freedom

"Freedom is not enough."
Lyndon B. Johnson

The gift of freedom requires my acknowledgment of the benefactor, God. To experience freedom without realizing its source is to miss the point; freedom requires responsibility.

When I was drinking, I demanded freedom without responsibility. I created my own horror stories. I hurt others because I did not respect in them what I demanded for myself, and slowly, ever so slowly, my freedom slipped away.

My spiritual program reinforces my responsibility for my life. God created me with free will, and I need to respect this gift in others. If I do not respect others, I will never receive it. Dignity is a two-way street.

Thank You for the freedom I experience
when I treat my neighbor with respect.

Life

"I am not afraid of tomorrow, for I have seen yesterday and I love today."
William Allen White

I have confidence in myself. I am experiencing consistency in my behavior and attitude. In recovery, things follow a natural progression, and life is more like a series of gentle curves than sharp peaks.

As an addict, my life was forever going up and down, ecstasy followed by gloom, the "best ever" followed by depression. It was always black or white, with no grays. Now things are connected, and I grow in the process of change. Sudden changes scare me because they are symptomatic of yesterday's disease and not consistent with the spiritual life I seek. Fortunately, I have the peace of knowing tomorrow will be something like today, and I am happy.

Thank You for the spiritual gift of consistency.

Pride

"The books I have not written are better than the books other people have."
Cyril V. Connolly

At times, I still grapple with pride, vanity, and conceit. Thanks to God and my spiritual program, I am not as preoccupied with self, but pride is still an obstacle sometimes because it keeps me isolated from others. It emphasizes the difference between me and the world, rather than the commonality. Pride keeps me a prisoner of ego and stops me from being grateful because it keeps me focused on what I am doing. In the process, I miss the beauty and splendor of my life. Pride keeps my nose pushed against the picture so I cannot see the portrait!

I can only change my prideful attitude by talking about it. The way for me to grow is to "dump it"—and do it today.

May I find myself in the people
I meet and with whom I share.

Forgiveness

"Forgiveness is the key to action and freedom."
Hannah Arendt

Early in sobriety, I found it easy to forgive others but hard to forgive myself. This kept me sick and negative because I was unable to practice self-love. I still blamed myself and felt responsible for being alcoholic. I had not surrendered to the reality of alcoholism as a disease.

Then a moment of sanity was granted in which I understood I was not responsible for being alcoholic but that I am responsible for my recovery. Recovery involves a healthy love and respect of self. This knowledge brings a tremendous joy and freedom that lead me to action in the recovering community. Only by loving myself will I be able to love others. In both these ways, I show my love for God.

May I always hold onto the
spiritual power of forgiveness.

Power

"The first and great commandment is, 'Don't let them scare you.'"
Elmer Davis

In sobriety, I still deal with fear. Fear of people, of not being good enough, of saying the wrong thing, or of not looking good enough still haunts me at times.

At the same time, my recovery tells me I am a child of God. I am a beautiful and powerful human being because not only did God make me but I share something of God's precious Divinity within myself. I am good enough. In God, I can afford to risk. Love must begin with my recognition of self.

Today I remember people are not "out to get me." I need not make myself the victim. People are much the same inside, and we all need each other to survive.

Thank You for the power to live
with my fear and grow from it.

Understanding

"Intelligence is proved not by ease of learning but by understanding what we learn."
Joseph Whitney

For years, I learned things without understanding what the words, or the meaning behind the words, really meant. An example was alcoholism. Then I heard someone say, "My name is Bill, and I'm an alcoholic and a recovering human being!"—and it struck me: recovery is not simply about putting down a substance but about developing a positive lifestyle as a human being.

The same is true with spirituality. It is not about religion, church, or dogma. It is about finding God in my life, discovering God in the decisions I make and actions I take, and seeing God in the world around me. Today I understand spirituality is centered on what is true and real.

*May I continue to search for
the harmony of understanding.*

Humility

"I believe the first test of a really great human being is humility."
John Ruskin

A definition of humility that makes sense to me is being aware of my limitations while still reaching for the stars. For years, I thought humility meant groveling in the dirt, keeping quiet, acting obsequiously, or being a doormat for others to walk on. Nothing could be further from the truth! Humility is about speaking my mind; fighting for my ideas and opinions; and creating alliances through effort, sweat, and debate. When I am truly humble, my ego is based in reality, not fed by illusion. When I am wrong, I can admit it and be open to the ideas of others.

Humility is based on a realistic self-love. Today I am willing to love myself, address my shortcomings, and grow in recovery.

God, let me humbly rejoice in
Your gift of creativity.

Tolerance

"Art, if it is to be reckoned with as one of the great values of life, must teach us . . . tolerance."
W. Somerset Maugham

There is something about art that is accepting, tolerant, and reconcilable with difference. I have observed that artists—those who paint, write, dance, sculpt, design, and think—are also accepting and tolerant because they need the different to create and progress. Things cannot stay the same. Art is the recorder of humankind's journey toward truth, but humankind needs friction, argument, confrontation, rejection—and yes, difference—to grow and develop.

In apparent difference, the seed of genius is often buried. Today I open my eyes and heart with acceptance. I become willing to be more tolerant of others and myself. I recognize beauty in all I observe.

God, before I reject someone as crazy,
let me seriously consider the message.

Art

"Art is not a thing; it is a way."
Elbert Hubbard

My Twelve Steps program talks about "a God of your own understanding." This is a liberating concept that teaches me to risk and think big. God is not only found in churches, temples, and rituals; God can be found in myriad art forms.

God is always present in the creative. Because art is always concerned with life and truth, God is always involved. Today I am able to look for God in God's world.

In my recovery from the disease of addiction, I am discovering the wonder and splendor of life that got damaged in my drinking days. Art inspires me to feel again. It helps me think and be concerned. Art teaches me to be involved in life.

Thank You for the beauty of art—
another aspect of spirituality.

Discovery

"I invent nothing. I rediscover."
Auguste Rodin

I believe spirituality is given to every human being, and I need only discover it in my life to experience its power. The history of my life has been more a circle than a straight line leading into the distance.

I am constantly returning to past events, reminiscences, and experiences that were part of my yesterdays but converge into my present. I am rediscovering yesterday in my every today; the fruits of my tomorrows are planted in the present moment.

My journey is not simply forward. It also involves a rediscovery of yesterday in today. My life is a mystery that exists within God.

With You, eternity is ever present,
and occasionally I get a glimpse of it.

Inferiority

*"I am the inferior of anyone whose rights
I trample underfoot."*
Horace Greeley

I recognize my feelings of inferiority in the arrogance of my past actions. Behind my pride was an incessant need to prove myself. My manipulative behavior was a cover for my insecurity. I had accepted I was not good enough, that I needed to pretend to be different. Alcohol abuse was part of the disease process. Money, friends, fast cars, and debts were all drawn into the delusion.

I am learning to accept me. Today I am happy. I can pay my bills. I have friends who love me. I no longer put others down to feel important. In sobriety, I have discovered the people I treated with disdain are just like me.

*May I receive healing and forgiveness
from those I considered inferior.*

Individuality

"I am one individual on a small planet in a little solar system in one of the galaxies."
Roberto Assagioli

Spirituality develops a humility in me that is realistic. Realism teaches me that I am one among many. That does not mean I am less than anybody else, but it certainly does not mean I am above others.

Arrogance, fantasy, and selfishness are characteristics of addiction that stop the development of individuality. Pretending to be something I am not or having a grandiose illusion about my own importance misses the truth of my individuality.

Humility means treating people with the respect I would want and giving people the freedom I require in my own life. Humility means perceiving my God-given talent and individuality.

Dear God, I pray I will remember I am a part rather than the sum total of this universe.

Majority

"One individual with courage is a majority."
Thomas Jefferson

Alcoholism made me afraid of my shadow. I became so paralyzed with fear I could not enjoy my life. I felt I could do nothing. My disease told me I was helpless. I existed in an atmosphere of doom and gloom.

Then I experienced a "moment" of sanity in which I recognized myself as the problem. My pain was caused by my own actions and attitudes. I took courage, confronted the disease, and decided to take small steps toward recovery.

I have built my confidence on that "moment" of courage. I am not an island unto myself. I am not alone. God is with me in my life, and so is my recovering community.

Give me courage to be what
You have created and accept my miracle.

Culture

"The great law of culture: Let each become all that he or she was created capable of being."
Thomas Carlyle

I am capable of great things. The history of humankind is the history of art, music, poetry, and romance. Each person, including me, is capable of great and noble acts—but do I want to do them?

The power of freedom and choice is the determining factor in my life. Every culture has imaginative and creative features, but nothing will happen in my life unless I make it so. The same is true of the culture of recovery. The people who make up the recovering community are the people who make a decision and act upon it. I must remember talk is cheap and cruel unless I follow it with an action. My decisions must be realistic. I always have the capacity to be honest and kind.

May I not only be grateful for my culture but live to add something to it.

Progress

"You must be a fool to want to stop the march of time."

Pierre Renoir

Fear of the future brought fear of change. My need to control made me avoid new or confusing ideas. My alcoholism wanted me to escape into the past; tomorrow was too fearful to contemplate.

At other times—and this is one of the reasons why alcoholism is cunning, baffling, and powerful—I wanted to escape into tomorrow and avoid the reality of today. Time and reality were concepts to be played with rather than experienced.

But time moves on, it progresses just like the disease, and if I want to be a winner in this world, I need to move with it. God is to be experienced in the march of time. Today I want to be in relationship with God.

Teach me to respect time
as an opportunity for growth.

Worship

"Our concern is not how to worship in the catacombs but how to remain human in the skyscrapers."
Abraham Joshua Heschel

Worship requires my discovery of true worth in my own life. True worship is not only historical and traditional but also contemporary. I need to discover not only the God of yesterday but also the God of the modern city.

My past addiction to fantasy often placed God in an unrealistic world. I was happy recognizing God among Jews, Romans, and Philistines, but I missed God in Las Vegas, on freeways, and in local politics.

My program has taught me that God is everywhere. Sobriety allows me to recognize God everywhere. God is alive in my world, and it would be tragic to make God a prisoner of history.

Let me find You in all the places I live.

Tact

"Tact is the art of making a point without making an enemy."
Howard W. Newton

Recovery entails not hurting people's feelings unnecessarily. I am learning to say what I have to say without causing offense. I am learning to be tactful and respectful.

As a drunk, I would say the first thing that came to mind, without regard for the feelings of others. I was often violent with words, sarcastic with comments, and cruel with dialogue. I judged tact as a sign of weakness. I regarded sensitivity as wimpy. I experienced my power by forcing people to change their minds!

Today I do not wish to live like this. I am willing to engage in sincere conversation. I am not afraid to show I care. Today I desire to be tactful.

God, let me always express
my opinion respectfully.

Observance

"The older I grow, the more I listen to people who do not say much."
Germain G. Glidden

In recovery, I enjoy watching others. I find the theater of life fascinating. I learn about myself by observing. I may identify with their mannerisms or facial expressions and intuitively sense their feelings. I sometimes recognize their fear, hesitancy, or shame and connect it with my own.

Recovery entails an instinctive spirituality that grows via observation. People are forever communicating—sending energy and messages—not only with words but by their existence, even by their silence. Sometimes, a person's silence can be deafening! God is alive for me in the lives of others, and part of my worship and prayer is observing the splendor and richness of my fellow and sister humans.

You who created the universe in magnificent silence, touch me with Your stillness.

Conscience

"In matters of conscience, the law of the majority has no place."
Mohandas K. Gandhi

So many times I caught myself pleasing the crowd, agreeing with people I did not understand or respect, laughing at jokes or opinions I loathed. How I used to hate myself!

Today I have a healthy respect for what the majority feels, but I also trust and follow my own conscience. I know to be in the minority is not necessarily to be in the wrong. Recovery insists that I listen to my conscience—the inner self that is based on a program of honesty, the spiritual cornerstone of my life I have come to trust. Now I can say to people "I do not agree." Today I give myself permission to disagree with family, friends, or colleagues.

May I never follow the crowd because
of the numbers, for You are one.

Unity

"This land of ours cannot be a good place for any of us to live unless we make it a good place for all of us to live."
Richard M. Nixon

Sobriety gives me a comprehensive view of life that includes my neighbor. We are all connected. If I hurt or am hurt, every person is affected at some level. Because we are all children of God, we are all one big family. We may speak different languages, observe different customs, display different physical characteristics, require different sexual and emotional satisfaction, but we are still one big family under God.

I have a responsibility to everyone in the family. I best exercise that responsibility by having a healthy respect for myself. I treat people as I would want to be treated, allowing them the freedom and love I require in my own life.

God, let me find my neighbor in myself.

Value

"A cynic is someone who knows the price of everything and the value of nothing."
Oscar Wilde

I did not know the value of my life until I looked beyond it. I was so self-obsessed that I missed the beauty of this world, so concerned with minutia that I missed the fun of living. I now see that my behavior had its roots in my childhood, in my dysfunctional family. I may have become a parent to my own parents. I took charge of everybody's life and felt responsible and guilty. Everything was work, and I did not learn how to play.

Now I am in recovery. I am dumping my feelings of guilt, shame, and anger. I am beginning to understand I am not responsible for my parents. I am beginning to feel free. Today I am learning to play!

Creator of the Divine dance, teach me Your steps.

Cynicism

"A cynic is one who, when he or she smells flowers, looks around for a coffin."
H. L. Mencken

There was a time I believed everyone was out to get me. I looked on the dark side of life. I was forever feeling negative and pessimistic. I was always surrounded by sick and destructive people.

When caring, healthy people offered hope or tried to help me, I turned away and rejected them. For years, I created the pain and misery in my own experience.

Then a close friend came into my life and gave me a dose of "tough love." This friend helped me see that I was wallowing in self-pity. This friend cared enough to intervene and tell me what I did not want to hear. Today I have time in recovery from alcoholism, and I carry the message to others.

May I always love myself and others enough to take a risk.

Flexibility

"Better bend than break."
Scottish Proverb

Dis-ease: controlling, stiff, and unbending. Sobriety: relaxed, comfortable, and flexible in my personal life and my interactions with others. Life: not a race or an exercise but an experience and an adventure. Before I accepted my alcoholism, I went through periods of "dryness." I stopped drinking to please others, rather than accepting the true nature of my disease. Everything was a premeditated act behind my mask of cheerfulness. I was angry, resentful, and in pain. Dryness is controlled denial.

Today the sobriety I have gained from my acceptance of self has overflowed into an acceptance of life on life's terms. Today I am happy.

Let the wind of experience bend me toward the knowledge of Your love.

Kindness

"Kindness in words creates confidence. Kindness in thinking creates profoundness. Kindness in giving creates love."
Lao Tzu

It costs me nothing to say hello, yet it can make a difference to my neighbor. It costs me nothing to give a hug, yet a hug can make a difference to a friend. It costs me nothing to listen to people's pain, yet listening can make a difference to them.

Love is found in small, ordinary acts of kindness, as well as extravagant gestures. I seek God in the everyday happenings of life alongside the religious events. Spirituality is in the smile that is real!

Today I know I give as much as I receive, and I receive a great deal. People love me enough to be patient, they care enough to phone, and they encourage me with gentle words of hope. I am in the flow.

You created the wondrous fabric of life.
May I find You in its smallest detail.

Justice

"Justice is truth in action."
Benjamin Disraeli

It is not enough for me to believe a thing is true; it is imperative that I live my beliefs. For too long, I held beliefs that kept me silent. My fear of displeasing others shaped my silent existence. Now I understand justice is part of spirituality. I need to walk as I talk! I am uncomfortable when I remain silent in the face of injustice. As a recovering alcoholic, such discomfort is dangerous because it can easily lead to low self-esteem, anger, resentment, and relapse.

Today I know I can slip without taking a drink. I may slip from where I want to be in my life. My personal integrity includes a definition of justice that can be seen in my lifestyle.

God of justice, teach me never again
to hide in the lie of silence.

Oratory

"The finest eloquence is that which gets things done."
David Lloyd George

I know how to talk. I know how to sound convincing. I know how to persuade a person as to my good intentions. Indeed such behavior was part of my manipulation for years.

Today I aim to walk the talk. I want to demonstrate what I say in the behavior I exhibit. The bottom line is action. Talking never stopped me from drinking; my physical refusal of the first drink was the start of my recovery.

God is to be discovered not merely in pious sentiments, as attractive as they may sound, but rather in the small steps of altered behavior. Am I doing what I am saying?

God, give me the courage to live my words.

Racism

"I want to be the white person's brother, not brother-in-law."
Martin Luther King, Jr.

Racism is about separation, ego, and isolation. So is addiction, and mine made me feel different. I covered my feelings with arrogance or false humility. Pride and inferiority put me on the defensive. I often sought a scapegoat for my anger. I was vindictive and prejudicial in my attitude toward others. It is a strange quirk of circumstance when one minority seeks to victimize another—and alcoholics are a minority group!

Sobriety is about a change in attitude and behavior. My spiritual acceptance of self inevitably leads to acceptance of others. The false pride and arrogance of my past give way to the vulnerable strength of sobriety. Now I embrace my neighbor, regardless of color, class, or creed.

God, teach me to seek You in my
fellow and sister humans.

Food

"Seeing is deceiving. It is eating that is believing."
James Thurber

For years, my belief system revolved around eating. I believed if I could eat, I always would be okay. Food was pleasure and escape for me. I lived to eat. Feelings—good or bad—were surrounded and stuffed down with food. I ate to avoid problems. Seeing was deceiving because I refused to accept the reality of my eating. I covered myself with clothes, avoided the beach, and rarely looked at my body. I saw only what I wanted to see—and I was dying.

Now I face reality. This is the meaning of spirituality. I show love for myself by loving food in a healthy way, making choices around what I eat, and eating slowly. Today I talk about my problems, rather than eating over them.

God, help me accept my daily bread
with gratitude and abstinence.

Saints and Sinners

"Every saint has a past and every sinner a future."
Oscar Wilde

I do not allow painful memories of my past to affect what I do today. Guilt is a killer if I allow it to have power. I have made amends. I have apologized to those I hurt. Today I begin the rest of my life.

The guilt and shame I felt for years grew out of my alcoholic behavior. As such, I need to remember I am not responsible for being alcoholic. It is not my fault. However, with the knowledge and acceptance of the disease comes a determination to live responsibly.

I have a sense of responsibility in my recovery. Spirituality means being a responsible person. The awareness and acceptance of my past can help create a loving future.

Infinite Spirit, show me how to
forgive myself and live in Your Love.

Risks

"Appeasers believe if you keep throwing steaks to a tiger, the tiger will become a vegetarian."
Heywood Broun

Spirituality involves risk, but the risk has to be sensible, having the possibility of success. As a practicing alcoholic, I risked extravagantly with no consideration of consequences. The decisions I make in recovery must be based on wisdom.

The risks I take today have a good chance of succeeding. Before taking action, I discuss the risk with a sponsor or recovering friend with time in sobriety.

Today I take risks on things and situations that have the possibility of working for me, rather than against me. God has given me freedom and has taken a risk on how I exercise that freedom. God's love is revealed in the risk. Risks should have the possibility of success!

God of wisdom, may I continue
to take sensible risks.

Solitude

"In solitude, be a multiple of thyself."
Tibullus

When I am alone and still, I get in touch with the side of me that includes "the many." As a child of God, I am a multifaceted individual.

There are many sides to me: the crazy and the sane, the extroverted and the introverted, the demanding and the submissive, the bigoted and the compassionate, the religious and the skeptical, the happy and the sad, the comical and the tragic, and the sick and the recovering. I embrace my total self with love and acceptance.

Today in the silence of solitude, I experience the many sides of myself. I choose to live fully and honor the contradictions. This is my spiritual reality.

May my varied experiences inform
my relationships with others.

Choices

"Another good reducing exercise consists in placing both hands against the table edge and pushing back."
Robert Quillen

I am an alcoholic. Today I choose not to drink. If alcohol is offered, I say "No." I do not go into "wet places," spend time with drinkers, or put myself in awkward situations. I support my own abstinence by the choices I make.

The recovering gambler avoids Las Vegas. The drug addict avoids sick relationships. The compulsive overeater must exercise the spiritual power of choice around food. "No" must involve both hands!

For the recovering person, talk must be accompanied by action. Some people, places, and things must be avoided. Today I am willing to love myself. In my awareness, I make the right choices to stay clean.

May my spirituality make my talk
a visible reality.

Teaching

"I hear and I forget. I see and I remember. I do and I understand."
Chinese Proverb

The best way for me to learn a thing is to do it, practice it, demonstrate it, and make it real. Spirituality must be experienced, not simply talked about. I cannot learn spirituality; I cannot get it from a guru or the latest self-help book.

Spirituality can only be discovered in the actual experiences of my life. It is found in my body, sexuality, sweat, anger, morning exercise, and kneeling in prayer and gratitude at the end of the day.

I am not an island. I cannot intellectualize recovery and expect it to grow. Spirituality is action. It is my experience of God in relation to myself and among other people. Today I rejoice in the gift of connection.

God, may You be real in my life.

Answers

"The spirit of liberty . . . is the spirit that is not too sure it is always right."
Judge Billings

I am free to make mistakes. It is okay for me to be wrong. I can say or do something that proves to be incorrect. I am not perfect.

Part of the liberty of being human is not being perfect. I am not God. In a sense, this is a relief. I do not have to take responsibility for the lives of others or the crises in the world. It is okay not to have all the answers. Indeed, the spiritual life is sometimes discovered in not knowing and allowing the answer to forever remain in the question.

My sobriety allows me to relax in any situation. It is perfectly human for me to ask "Why am I like I am?" But the answer rests in God.

God of reason, let me be satisfied
with discovering You in the questions.

Belief

"An atheist is one who has no invisible means of support."
John Buchanan

The common cry of those who suffer from addiction is that they feel isolated from self, family, friends, and God. I, too, felt alone in my addiction. Behind my feelings of isolation were teachings and attitudes that produced guilt, shame, and fear. I viewed God as the hammer with which society beats the addict.

Today, in an atmosphere of love and support, I begin to look at these old attitudes and, hopefully, begin to change them. God can be seen in a hug as well as a sacrament, in doubt as well as dogma.

In the honest sharing of fellow and sister addicts, God is made known to me. God needs to be given a human face.

Teach me to grow in the virtues
of tolerance and understanding.

Fear

"A good scare is worth more to us than good advice."
Ed Howe

My fear of alcoholism helped move me into treatment. My awareness of reality—"I am an alcoholic"—helped me move toward recovery. I was literally scared into healing! I must never forget my frightening yesterdays because doing so could easily lead to minimization and tomorrow's denial. I need to remember my pain if I am to gain. My inappropriate behavior, my abuse of self and others, and my feelings of self-loathing should be reckoned with, on a daily basis, because they are only one drink away!

God has given me a memory, and I need to use it. My spiritual courage is in remembering my yesterdays so I can continue to enjoy my sobriety today.

May I recognize that healthy fear
comes from You; it is part of Your love for me.

Thought

"There is no place in active life on which thought is negligible."
T. S. Eliot

It is not a crime to think. It is not a sin to have a brain. To think is human. Unfortunately, much of my past thinking was destructive and negative. The disease of addiction permeated every aspect of my life, particularly my thoughts. For years, my best ideas justified my addiction.

Today I am open to a change of mind. I choose to change my ideas. I am free to think differently. I focus on thoughts of healing. My recovering community supports me with acceptance and love.

God is alive in my willingness to change. I am blessed with allies who are also walking the path. Together, we think and grow in the light of sobriety.

God, help my thinking recover.

Acceptance

"Adversity is the trial of principle. Without it, one hardly knows whether one is honest or not."
Henry Fielding

Acceptance of my disease brought me recovery. If I had not recognized and confronted my addiction, I would not know the joy of sobriety and serenity. Spirituality involves facing my disease.

Because I did not see my dishonesty, I could not fully appreciate honesty. If I had not recognized my lies and games, I could not have appreciated the openness and freedom of sobriety. Owning my violence brought me to peace and tolerance. Facing my hell gave me a glimpse of paradise. The disease was my prison, but when I accepted it, it became my key to recovery. Finding God in my life requires a rigorous honesty in which I use the pain of the past to experience gratitude today.

God, it is through the acceptance of my failings that I can love the world.

Faith

"Faith is never identical with piety."
Karl Barth

Drugs created a world of fantasy rather than a life of reality. Everything was exaggerated and dehumanized, especially my practice of spirituality. For the addict, religion often becomes part of the escape. Ritual may become theatrical, leading one to expect magic rather than a miracle. Icons are worshipped, promises are made, confessions become routine, prayers are mouthed, and God is manipulated.

Piety, the religious art of showmanship, kept me prisoner to a small god. Faith, on the other hand, takes my pain and isolation seriously and promises recovery only when I change and accept responsibility. I must walk my prayers and live my rituals!

God, build Your temple in my heart,
Your altar on my love of self and others.

Peace

"Peace without justice is tyranny."
William Allen White

Peace at any price is not a maxim I adopt. For years, I was seeking a peace based on the "no-talk" principle—remaining quiet rather than causing upset or risking embarrassment. Such peace was unjust. It fed my disease and helped keep me sick.

Today I seek a peace that involves discussing or confronting painful situations. This may make me or others uncomfortable, and that is okay. Serenity is peace achieved after periods of necessary pain.

Now I have the courage to speak out and make choices that are good for me. I do so from a place of truth and integrity. I speak from my sense of conviction with love. God is always alive in my choices.

May I forever know the peace that is real.

Religion

"It is the test of a good religion if you can joke about it."

G. K. Chesterton

Today I am able to joke with God and about God. Today I am able to laugh with me about me. Laughter is one of the greatest gifts I have received in my journey of sobriety.

In my recovering community, I laugh with my brothers and sisters. I share their joy, and I share their pain. My spirituality comes alive in the company of clean and sober people.

Today I am able to laugh in a healthy way about God, the Church, spirituality, and recovery. Laughter joyously reflects my human imperfection and at the same time reminds me of God's glory embodied in my life.

*God, I contemplate You laughing
at my pompous piety.*

Money

"Money does not always bring happiness. People with ten million dollars are no happier than people with nine million dollars."
Hobart Brown

There is nothing intrinsically wrong with money. It is not good or bad in itself—it is what I do with it. As a comedian stated, "I've been rich and I've been poor. Rich is better!" In what sense is it better? Perhaps in the freedom it affords me to travel or buy things, or in the way I can help others and contribute to their well-being. To hoard money, be stingy with myself or others, make a god of possessions, or be compulsive about earning produces the same pain as any other addiction.

Money is meant to be used. It is a benefit of sobriety, part of what it means to say "It gets better." Sober, I am more responsible and creative, and this brings its rewards.

Help me be a responsible steward
of the possessions You entrust to me.

Leisure

"It is seldom an American retires from business to enjoy fortune in comfort.... We work because we have always worked and know no other way."
Thomas Nichols

For years, I rushed around being busy—and I missed me. I spent far too much time trying to please people by doing things—and I missed me. I was a workaholic whose only value was in what I could achieve—and I missed me.

Today I can relax in my sobriety because sobriety has enabled me to relax. I can sit and do nothing and it is okay. Life is about "being," not "doing." Spirituality is about taking time out for me because I am worth it. "Be still and know that I am God," wrote the psalmist.

In the silence of self, I have discovered the meaning of life. I have found God. In my leisure, I pause to appreciate these gifts.

Thank You for creating the feelings of peace that come from leisure.

Comfort

"No one knows of what stuff one is made until prosperity and ease try one."
A. P. Gouthey

I must not get too comfortable or self-confident. I must not plateau at this stage of sobriety. I cannot afford to relax in past achievements. Sometimes, I hear my addiction saying "You've done all you need. Relax and take it easy." Other times, the sick voice commands, "Listen to the stupidity of these newly recovering people. Avoid them! You don't need meetings now."

Based on my experience, when things are going well I need to be careful. A complacent sobriety is dangerous. It leads to the disarming slip of arrogance and false pride. I need to remember the pain of my yesterdays and keep listening to the newly recovering.

*Teach me to embrace humility
and enjoy a realistic sobriety.*

Friendship

"True friendship comes when silence between two people is comfortable."
Dave Tyson Gentry

A spiritual practice that awakens serenity includes silence and stillness. "Be still and know that I am God." True friendship is Divine. It is a special love that binds two hearts as one. It is the opposite of dis-ease.

Friendship is necessary to recovery and involves sharing feelings. Often the feelings are silent: unspoken emotions, cherished moments that exist in wordlessness. As a recovering alcoholic, I have a thousand friends who attest to the silent witness of love by simply being there. They are my allies. They are my friends.

Sobriety allows me to communicate without speech when the situation calls for it. Seeing God in the eyes of others tells me more than words could ever say.

Thank You for the joy of friendship
that grows in silence.

Experience

"Experience is not what happens to us. It is what we do with what happens to us."
Aldous Huxley

I feel the joy of sobriety. I see God in my world. I know the peace and serenity that eluded me for years. Experience is a key to my recovery. It locates all that is tangible in my life. It allows me to appreciate what living is all about.

Love is meant to be felt. Forgiveness is meant to be experienced. Humility is meant to be lived in action. Hope is meant to be recognized in the brightness of the eyes. My spirituality entails the lived experience of God working in my world. Recovery is not something I can merely intellectualize—I must walk the talk. Joy should not be limited to the imagination—I want to feel it. Today I live my dream as experienced reality.

Loving Creator, may my experience
of You be reflected in my daily life.

Strength

"All cruelty springs from weakness."
A Seneca Saying

Spiritual recovery means I must confront my disease and remember the sick attitudes and behavior patterns. Sometimes, I would rather not talk about my disease for it can be embarrassing and shameful, particularly the cruelty I demonstrated. Alcoholism made me lash out at the weak. My own weakness inflicted pain and cruelty on others.

Today I remember this only to rejoice in the strength that allows me vulnerability. My past weaknesses made me act as if I were strong. Now my strength allows me to be weak in a way that is healthy.

I get my ego out of the way and open my heart to love. I know my strength is God ordained and shows up in myriad ways.

God, the recognition of my past cruelties enables me to forgive and understand others.

Forgiving

"One that cannot forgive others breaks the bridge over which one must pass oneself, for every person has need to be forgiven."
Thomas Fuller

My failings as an alcoholic help me accept others. The fact that I make mistakes helps me enjoy creative relationships. Because I know what it means to fail, I understand the failings of others. My weaknesses are a bridge to my fellow and sister human beings.

By contrast, when I was drinking I thought I was perfect. I always had to be right, which led to judgment, argument, and alienation. Alcohol fed my arrogance and pride; sobriety nurtures my humility and understanding.

Today I am comfortable in my skin. I allow others, and myself, all the latitude necessary to grow. My recovery expands as I forgive.

God, I understand that even my
failings can work for me in sobriety.

Yesterdays

"When I want to understand what is happening today or try to decide what will happen tomorrow, I look back."
Oliver Wendell Holmes Jr.

The writing is on the wall! My writing is on my wall and can be seen in my life! The history of my life teaches me about my alcoholism. Alcoholism is a personal disease; it affects others through the individual self. Sometimes, I am tempted to forget the past. Why live in yesterday? While I recover by living in today, I must understand how the events of yesterday affect my present.

The future is forged by my recognition of the past. My disease grew strong in denial. Recovery begins with acceptance of reality. Today does not exist in a vacuum. Tomorrow is determined by the decisions I make now. I know my recovering life demands a true recognition of yesterday.

Thank You for the historical progression of my recovery.

Heroes

"Self-trust is the essence of heroism."
Ralph Waldo Emerson

In recovery, I have become my own hero. It may sound egotistical, but it is part of my program of self-love. I may have other heroes, but today I respect myself.

I believe that God is involved in my life. An aspect of Divinity exists within me. I trust myself with my own life. I am proud of the daily choices I make in the best interest of my sobriety.

Spirituality allows me to be my own hero because it is with respect of self that I can truly respect others. My awareness of dignity affords dignity to others. My personal healing brings healing to others. Today I am the center of my universe, and I shine my light everywhere.

Thank You for the achievements and successes in my life. Today I am my own winner.

Overeating

"Obesity is really widespread."
Joseph O. Kern II

To overeat compulsively is to be lost. It is the result of addiction, like alcoholism and drug abuse. Compulsive overeating and other eating disorders are widespread. Sometimes they manifest as one recovers from another addiction. Cross addiction would be a tragedy for me. Today I stay focused and aware. I reach out to others and avoid isolation. I may be tempted to overeat or abuse sugar, but this can be changed. People can and do recover from food compulsion by surrendering to reality.

My people-pleasing must be addressed. Feelings I bury behind food must be expressed. Recovery happens when I love and believe in myself.

Dear God, You hear the prayers of all
Your children; please hear my prayers, too.

Memories

"History is the seedbed of the future."
Leo Booth

I talk about my drinking history because there is no gain without pain. To enjoy sobriety, I must share the reality of my disease. My pain is rooted in my history. I must live with my disease on a daily basis and be aware of the disease process in my life. This awareness requires a rigorously honest inventory of my past attitudes and behaviors. Ignorance is bliss for the disease of addiction!

Awareness and acceptance of my past are my treatment for today. My life has a history, and my spiritual program demands I understand it. While I do not wallow in the past, I recognize its influence on my present and how it informs my future.

Teach me to face my past so
I can realistically live in today.

Shame

"If we are not ashamed to think it, we should not be ashamed to say it."
Marcus Tullius Cicero

I was afraid to tell others what I thought. I was afraid to speak or be noticed. I sat for hours in silence. At times, I wished I could vanish into the furniture. I was afraid of my shadow.

This reveals not only my lack of confidence but also my low self-esteem. I did not think I had anything to offer that might be interesting. I would laugh at stupid things to please people.

Today I speak out with courage. I do not hide what I am thinking. I believe I have something to offer in the celebration of life. And it feels good! My spiritual growth is proportionate to my willingness to let others know who I am and what I think.

May I celebrate my joy in living by sharing it.

Idealism

"I am an idealist. I do not know where I am going, but I am on my way."
Carl Sandburg

Today I am on the move. I feel a new energy in my life that brings excitement to each day. New people, new places, and new ideas give me a spiritual charge that helps me enjoy my life.

I do not have all the answers and am sometimes confused, but today I can live with this and enjoy it. God seems to be revealed more in the questions than the answers. It is often my problems that produce the most growth.

The journey of my life is an adventure that is free and uncharted. Even the pain and problems produce a benefit I can use for my recovery. Nothing need be wasted.

You are the Way, the Truth, and the Light.
May I always walk with You.

Recovery

"There is a destiny that makes us brothers; none goes his way alone. All that we send into the lives of others come back into our own."
Edwin Markham

I remember feeling isolated and alone. I watched people talking with friends, families playing in the park, and lovers holding hands, and I felt different and awkward. I always looked at life from the outside. I was the one without an invitation to the party. Such are the symptoms of addiction! My behavior around alcohol reinforced negative and destructive feelings. By drinking, I perpetuated the painful disease in my life.

Sobriety brings me into comradeship with others, into the family of recovering people. Now I am not alone. I have over a million brothers and sisters living a day at a time in a spiritual program. Today I belong in this world.

Thank You for the need
to give so that I might receive.

Opportunity

"Whenever science makes a discovery, the devil grabs it while the angels are debating the best way to use it."
Alan Valentine

Sometimes I spend so long deciding what to do that I miss the opportunity. I can fabricate outcomes to the point of impotence. Nowhere is this truer than in relationships. I see someone I like and go home thinking about what I could have said or done. I create happenings in my mind that never happened in fact. I miss the spiritual opportunity of risk.

For years I behaved this way. I always thought I was not good enough, not important enough. The syndrome of low self-esteem convinced me I was less than other people. Today it is better. My growth includes reaching out to others. I make a point of saying hello. I have the courage to risk a friendship or relationship.

Let me not debate myself
into sickness and isolation.

Certainty

"The certainties of one age are the problems of the next."
R. H. Tawney

At times, I was a religious bigot. I did not know, but now I see how closed and narrow my thinking was. I craved certainty because I felt it would give me security and happiness—but it never did. I argued dogmas I did not believe; such is the plight of the unhappy hypocrite!

Today I live only in the certainty of the moment. I know what worked for me yesterday will work for me today if I am open to love, truth, honesty, and change. Change is not necessarily difference if I see it as part of a process rather than as an isolated event. The one thing of which I can be certain is change. The God of truth is revealed in change; my acceptance of this fact is spirituality in action.

*May I grow in the spiritual life
by my desire to change and be tolerant.*

Trust

"We become civilized, not in proportion to our willingness to believe, but in our readiness to doubt."

H. L. Mencken

A civilized nation is a spiritual nation. A civilized person is one who seeks truth and is willing to change. I want to be such a person living in such an environment.

Sobriety is adventurous because it is bigger than simply not drinking. Recovery seeks to address all areas of my life and all situations. An example is trust. When I was drinking, I trusted no one because I felt everybody was like me—that is, out for themselves and therefore not trustworthy.

Today I know the real enemy in my life is me. I am the one who brings pain into my life. But now I am beginning to love myself by my decision not to drink. Today I am willing to trust.

Spirit of truth, help me
freely trust others and myself.

Fate

"I am the master of my fate; I am the captain of my soul."
William E. Henley

Things do not just happen; I make them so. For years, I thought getting well depended on my family getting well. I rooted my recovery in the recovery of others. I was the typical codependent.

Then somebody said, "Why don't you start taking responsibility for your own life?" I thought about that remark for weeks. I am sure I had heard a similar sentiment a hundred times, but that night, that special night, I was ready to hear it. That was a spiritual moment.

Today I believe such spiritual moments produce a spiritual process I must keep alive. I am the deciding factor in what happens to me and what I achieve. God created me to be involved in my recovery.

May I always steer my life
in the direction of truth and love.

December

Gossip

"Great minds discuss ideas, average minds discuss wants, and small minds discuss people."
Laurence J. Peter

Gossip is a form of malicious cowardice. It is blasphemy because it denigrates human beings made in God's image.

As a practicing alcoholic, I was a gossip. I exaggerated and manipulated the truth with my gossip. I made up stories against people toward whom I held resentments. Innocent people were abused and victimized by my gossip. I also loved listening to gossip. The listener plays an important role in the life of gossip because without someone to listen, it could not be perpetuated. It takes two to gossip!

Today gossip is unacceptable behavior in my program. I regard my fellows and sisters with respect. I refrain from causing damage with my words.

*Teach me to reach beyond
my smallness into Your greatness.*

Problems

"The certainties of one age are the problems of the next."

R. H. Tawney

Life is a process that sometimes entails problems. Fear of the new, discomfort with old values being seen as wrong, and confusion that often accompanies growth are a few examples.

As an alcoholic, I tried to run away from problems by drinking. But the next day, the old problems were still there, and my drinking usually brought new ones in addition. Alcohol produced a momentary escape, but reality always returned.

Today with the acceptance of my alcoholism and my decision not to pick up the first drink, I face problems courageously and deal with them wisely. I live with the problems of life and do not allow them to spoil my existence.

Teach me to joyously accept
any problems life and growth may bring.

Wonder

"Wonder rather than doubt is the root of knowledge."
Abraham Joshua Heschel

Living with paradox is part of sobriety. Things are never quite what they seem. Just when I think I have something figured out, I find I am confused again—especially around life, relationships, people, events, and the universe.

Life is simple yet incomprehensible. God seems to demand an agnostic faith! There is so much I do not know or understand.

Fortunately, this leads to a creative and exciting sobriety. It makes my life an adventure. It feeds that artistic part of me that is reborn in sobriety. Things I used to dislike when I drank, I now enjoy. People and writers who once bored me now fascinate me. Everything has a spiritual message!

God, let feelings of amazement
always be part of my faith.

Prejudice

"Everyone is a prisoner of his or her own experiences. No one can eliminate prejudices—just recognize them."
Edward R. Murrow

In recovery, I am accepting that I am not perfect. Some prejudices are part of my life—what it is to be human. On a daily basis, I am trying to deal with prejudice, and talking about it helps. Judgment does not go away just because I talk about it, but I do get a better perspective and grow in an understanding of myself through the recognition of my prejudices.

Alcoholism made me a fake: I appeared to be what I was not, and my prejudices were part of the camouflage. My prejudices revealed my fears and my need to people-please. Slowly, in my daily spiritual program, I am discovering the courage to stand alone.

Teach me to love truth more than popularity.

Beauty

"Not everyone in old slippers can manage to look like Cinderella."
Don Marquis

Beauty is not how I look; it is within. I began to love myself when I saw the beauty God has given everyone—including me. God's image expresses through my attitudes and feelings, in how I greet and listen to others, and in the gentle dignity I afford them.

For years, I saw myself as ugly, boring, and stupid. This message came from parents who forever compared me with others, and I believed them. I hid through my teenage years and quietly tried to escape in food, alcohol, or drugs. Then I met people who had felt the same but were now feeling different. They loved me until I could begin to love myself. Today I can love others as well.

*Help me see beauty in the wrinkle
and power in the pain.*

Failure

"There are two kinds of failures: those who thought and never did, and those who did and never thought."
Laurence J. Peter

In my own life, I know I am guilty of both these failures. I remember making sandcastles in the air without realizing I could build one in my life. I would see somebody I wanted to talk with and imagine a conversation, rather than going over and risking possible rejection.

Today I am able to risk. I am now the possessor of a thousand memories that actually happened.

I am also aware of how thoughtless I was in my addiction. I would react rather than respond, creating hostility as a wall to keep people out. Today I am able to think through a problem and apologize when I am wrong.

God, help me accept the
richness of life on life's terms.

Reality

"Humans are complex beings: they make deserts bloom and lakes die."
Gil Stern

I am a mix of good and bad. When I was drinking, I could be cruel, sarcastic, and violent but at other times loving, sensitive, and thoughtful. In recovery, I can be honest, humble, and creative, but I also harbor a dark side that may hurt, lie, or seek negative power. What a mix I was and still am! In my many conversations with a variety of people, I have discovered this is part of what it means to be human.

Now I am able to accept this fact and develop my spiritual life. I am not perfect, but I try to improve my attitude and behavior. I am not God, but I can aspire to be the best I can be. Today I own the sickness in my life, but I also accept the responsibility for recovery.

With my feet in the dirt, I look to the stars.

Enjoyment

"All animals, except humans, know the ultimate of life is to enjoy it."
Samuel Butler

Today I choose to enjoy life. Regardless of any problems or difficulties this day may bring, I am blessed with an inner joy that comes with my recovery from addiction.

With a clear head and body—free from drugs and chemicals—I can face today and look forward to tomorrow. My life is to be enjoyed, not endured. My worst days in recovery are better than my best days as an addict.

Spiritually, I am free because I have begun to discover myself. I now perceive God in every dimension of my world because I have sobriety.

Creator of all play, I dance before You in my world and I stop to smell the roses.

Aging

"Growing old is not so bad when you consider the alternative."
Maurice Chevalier

What is the alternative to aging? Not to change! To stay rooted in adolescence, youth, middle age, or whatever age and refuse to grow. Not to age is not to live, experience, or grow spiritually.

An aspect of age for which I am grateful is comparison. Today I am able to look at the past and see the benefits of the present. Growth is measurable only through the tunnel of age. I suppose my fear of age is my basic fear of the unknown, fear of unmanageability and powerlessness.

These words remind me of the spiritual program that teaches me to confidently place my life in the loving arms of God. If I am responsible in life, I will be responsible at any age.

Teach me to use the spiritual perspective that comes with the gift of age.

Service

"There is no higher religion than human service. To work for the common good is the greatest creed."
Albert Schweitzer

I enjoy doing things for other people. I enjoy knowing other people are happy. I enjoy seeing gratitude in their eyes and experiencing their hugs of thankfulness.

Some people need to restrict how much they do for others and begin doing more for themselves. I, on the other hand, am happy and pleased with my service for others because I used to only be a taker. For years, as a practicing alcoholic, I would walk away with all someone could give me and only thank them because I wanted to return for more!

In sobriety, I am beginning to change this. Now I am giving and enjoying it.

God, the gift of service is a precious gift.

Today

"The only courage that matters is the kind that gets you from one moment to the next."
Mignon McLaughlin

I do not need courage for a lifetime—just for the moment. I am helped by the philosophy that teaches me to live one day at a time, one hour at a time, or one moment at a time. It is too daunting to try to live tomorrow. Life is a process to be lived, not a future to be anticipated.

For years, I tried to anticipate what life would throw at me, and I always came away confused and exhausted. I missed the joy of the moment. I had a thousand questions I could not answer; nobody can answer for the future today.

I can only take responsibility for my life a day at a time. As I develop the courage to face the moment, I become a winner.

May I avoid the fantasy of tomorrow
and enjoy the reality of today.

Principles

"At the back of every noble life are the principles that have fashioned it."
Geoorge Lorimer

God is found in principles—the suggested patterns of behavior that lead to happiness, freedom, and unity in the world. God is not just an intellectual philosophy or otherworldly entity; God is practical goodness that can be demonstrated and seen in my world.

Principles produce changes in my attitude and behavior and lead me to positive action. Principles must have a practical result. I often hear the phrase "Walk the talk," meaning the principles I talk about in recovery should be evident in my daily life. Principles should also be seen in the small things: being courteous, smiling at a stranger, or offering a hug to a friend in pain. God is alive in the principles of life.

Help me practice the principles I believe.

Suffering

*"We cannot remake ourselves without suffering,
for we are both the marble and the sculptor."*
Alexis Carrel

I know I have grown through my suffering. I know I
am able to understand and forgive other people
because I have been there, too. I know I am patient and
considerate as a result of my suffering.

My anguish keeps me grounded. It stops me from
playing God and teaches me the reality of life. Sometimes, that reality is that life hurts! And life is also wonderful, joyous, loving, and eventful.

For many years, I hid my suffering and pretended it
was not there. The result was loneliness and hypocrisy.
Today I remake myself with courage and gratitude.

God, may my suffering keep me real.

God

"My God, my God, why hast thou forsaken me?"
Matthew 27:46

In my sickness, I was often angry with God. I was angry because God did not do what I wanted when I wanted it done. I acted like a spoiled child. I refused to understand that suffering could be an important part of my spiritual growth.

Today I know this to be true, and I appreciate it. The biggest part of my suffering, then and now, is the feeling of isolation: not knowing for certain if God hears me, not understanding completely what God's will is for me, or not getting clear answers to my daily confusion.

Doubt is part of faith. The "not knowing" is sometimes the answer. Today I trust in God as I focus on my recovery.

God, may my doubts lead to creative faith.

Poverty

"The poor you always have with you."
John 12:8

Great numbers of people live in circumstances beyond their control and die in poverty. The poor are always with us. I cannot understand this dilemma, and I have few answers for most of the world's suffering. However, I have faith in God's love being realized for everyone.

Many are spiritually destitute by their own making. This was my reality when I drank. I chose to live a life that was consistently destructive, and I refused to change. Alcoholics and drug addicts are committing suicide by their behavior! I know, because for years I was a practicing one. This produces a spiritual poverty that can be overcome. Recovery is finding the hidden treasure within.

Let me find Your treasure
in the loving care I give myself.

Generosity

"Liberty is the one thing you cannot have unless you give it to others."
William Allen White

Spirituality is rooted in a respect for self that demands an equal respect for others. I can expect to be treated with dignity if I afford dignity to others. In the one lies the key to the many.

For years, I lived a compulsive life that only made me self-centered and spoiled—and it didn't work! I was unhappy, lonely, and resentful. In recovery, I have realized I need others and others need me. Together, we grow in the spirit of generous sharing.

Today I find that the more I give to others, the more I receive. Less is often more. In this sense, it is much easier to be good than bad, because goodness works!

Spirit of generosity, may I always
reflect the gratitude that gives.

Fear

"Nothing in life is to be feared. It is only to be
understood."

Marie Curie

God is on my side. I believe this truth, and it helps me
cope with my fears. Now I understand I was the
only real enemy in my life. With my new perspective on
God, I have the power of choice. I do not have to stay in
a sick process. I do not need sick people in my life. I do
not have to place myself in destructive relationships or
fearful situations. God is alive in my life, and I have the
spiritual power of choice.

I am no longer crippled by fear. The God of my own
understanding works for me. I am blessed with friends
and allies in my recovering community who support my
growth. There is nothing in my life to be feared and
much to be celebrated.

God, give me the courage to confront
fear and make changes in my life.

Freedom

"You are free and that is why you are lost."
Franz Kafka

Part of spirituality is having many choices and living in moments of not knowing. Part of being human is sometimes feeling lost. These feelings can lead to fear and loneliness, or they can be seen as the essence of risk and adventure.

With freedom comes uncertainty. In reality, nothing is predestined or made to happen—God is in my choices. I do not have all the answers. I am not sure of the results. My joy is mingled with pain and sorrow. Such is the divinity of life, and I choose to live!

Sobriety is accepting the reality of uncertainty in my life. My responsibility is accepting this freedom and making a daily choice not to drink.

May I accept feeling lost, knowing
I am found in You.

Individuality

*"The People, though we think a great entity when
we use the word, means nothing more than so
many millions of individual men and women."*
James Bryce

I am an individual. I am unique. I am special. Today I
am able to enjoy my difference. I do not need to hide
in alcohol, food, or drugs. I do not have to put energy
into being the same as my friends or neighbors. I do not
need to please others to feel good about myself. Today I
am my own person.

God made people varied and different in many ways,
yet so many of us spend our time trying to be the same.
The effort I exerted to achieve the lowest common
denominator was exactly that—the lowest. My spiritual
program demands that I be honest with who I am and
what I feel. My self-worth is rooted in my individuality.
In my difference lies my soul.

*Eternal One, may I always
remain true to my individuality.*

Pessimism

"Pessimist: One who, when given the choice of two evils, chooses both."
Oscar Wilde

In the past, I always looked on the gloomy side of life. The glass was always half empty. I remember thinking nothing good was ever going to happen, life was to be endured, everybody had a price, and people were all selfishly looking out for themselves.

I projected onto others my own sickness, my own despair, and my own pessimism. In that regard, mine was a suicidal existence.

Today I choose to be a positive and creative person who refuses to be surrounded by negativism. My attitude in life makes all the difference as to my enjoyment of life. Now my glass is more than half full, and I am happy.

God, in the gift of choice,
may I recognize my potential joy.

Orginality

"Originality exists in every individual because each of us differs from the other. We are all primary numbers divisible only by ourselves."
Jean Guitton

For too many years, I tried to be the same as other people. I matched their styles, repeated their words, and did what they wanted.

I lived to please a crowd of people I did not really know—and they certainly did not know me! I recited other people's prayers, quoted other people's opinions, and memorized others' ideas—and I felt empty.

Today I value the lives of others, and I am beginning to explore my place in the universe. I accept the "specialness" that is me, that uniqueness that makes me one of God's miracles. Now others are listening to what I say and benefiting from my life.

God, in my difference I am discovering my service.

Perseverance

"Great works are performed not by strength, but perseverance."
Samuel Johnson

Today I saw a staggering drunk in a parking lot. Last night in a meeting, I witnessed a frail person celebrate ten years of sobriety. The difference? Perseverance. People always get what they really want in life.

If I want sobriety more than anything else and am prepared to go to any lengths, nothing will stop me. Perseverance reveals the "walk" as well as the "talk."

Today I need to remember that what is worth having may require sacrifice and effort. God helps those who are prepared to help themselves. Today I intend to help myself to sobriety.

May I always persevere
through my fears toward my goals.

Language

"If thought corrupts language, language can also corrupt thought."
George Orwell

Sobriety means much more than not drinking or not using. It means the daily decision to be a positive and creative human being in all areas of my life: how I treat people, what I eat, the books I read, and how I speak!

Not even my worst enemy would call me a prude, but inappropriate language, used on a regular basis, is unacceptable in my sobriety. Why? Because it hurts the listener and does not show respect for myself or the God-given gift of communication.

If I have no respect for language, I will ultimately not grow as a spiritual person. Today I am mindful of my language as part of my recovery.

May Your words of love always be reflected in my language.

Comradeship

"I am a citizen, not of Athens or Greece, but of the world."

Socrates

Recovery helps me see that I belong—not simply to a race or nation but to the world! The freedom I experience in sobriety allows me to embrace all cultures, races, and religions. Spirituality has brought harmony into my life.

I can go where I please. I can learn languages and communicate with people in foreign lands. I can listen to ideas that enrich my understanding of God. My healing in recovery is more than discovering choice around alcohol; it is discovering choice around life.

Today I choose to live life fully. I go forward into my day and meet the eyes of every person with love, as if to say "Welcome to my world!"

God of wholeness, may I always see
and appreciate the richness of my life.

Generosity

"And the Word was made flesh and dwelt amongst us."
John 1:14

There once was a land where everyone had abundant "warm fuzzies" they exchanged and shared. Everything was wonderful because all people gave and received generously. A rumor began that there was a shortage of warm fuzzies, and people began to selfishly protect their supply. Then "cold pricklies" were introduced. Sadness, persecution, and pain developed as the growth of cold pricklies kept people fearful and alone.

The tragedy is that the rumor was not true! As long as I generously share my warm fuzzies, they will never disappear. My gifts and talents only disappear when they are not shared. The more I give, the more I receive.

Creator, may I always be
generous with all You have given me.

Apathy

"The only thing necessary for the triumph of evil is for good people to do nothing."
Edmund Burke

I read about the Holocaust, and I am ashamed to belong to the human race, which allowed, by an overwhelming silence, the slaughter of millions. The ultimate mode of people-pleasing is to do nothing. Power is an addiction rarely discussed. Evil needs people and politics to function; alone, it is but a concept.

I know evil because I know myself. I know tyranny and injustice because for years I perpetrated negativity. Now I choose to say "No." Today I seek to make amends for past wrongs by being rigorously honest in all my affairs. Because I know what it is to hate, I seek to love. I wish to be responsible in God's world.

God of love, teach me to learn
from my mistakes and translate
that knowledge into action.

Lies

"Sin has many tools, but a lie is the handle that fits them all."
Oliver Wendell Holmes

Lying robs life of meaning. In my addiction, I was a liar, not just by what I said, but by what I did, what I left unsaid, and by my manipulation with half-truths.

As a liar, I was forced into the prison of loneliness, despair, and isolation because nobody could know or understand me. My language and communication were ego centered. I was not living in the real world. I was living in my own world with my own rules and definitions. The lies were the killing wounds, and they were self-inflicted.

Today I prefer the pain of truth to the passing satisfaction of lies. The healthy habit of telling the truth is growing in me!

Spirit of truth, may You ever be reflected in the life I seek to live.

Humor

"Humor is an affirmation of dignity, a declaration of one's superiority to all that befalls one."
Romain Gary

Today I laugh at myself. I need to laugh at myself to stay sane. I choose not to take myself too seriously.

When I tell jokes about the alcoholic, I am not belittling the person; rather, I am making fun of the disease that nearly killed me. For me to live with the disease, I need to be able to laugh at it. In this way, I stop alcoholism from having power in my life.

In addition, I catch something of the symptoms of the disease in my jokes: the grandiosity, arrogance, manipulation, insanity, ego, selfishness, and exaggeration. Joking allows me to face reality with a smile. Today I use humor in a loving and mindful way.

God, thank You for the healing gift of humor.

Madness

"The madman who knows he is mad is close to sanity."
Juan Ruiz de Alarcón

Alcoholics who continue to drink, addicts who continue to use, and overeaters who continue to eat compulsively are committing suicide. This is pure madness; it is like stabbing yourself with a knife and asking "Why am I bleeding?" The definition of insanity is repeating the same behavior and expecting a different result. Today I behave as a person in recovery behaves; I do what is necessary to stay sober for twenty-four hours. And I fully expect to be successful.

I accept my past destructive behavior and aim to change it on a daily basis. Spirituality is loving myself enough to see the writing on the wall and do something about it.

God, You seem to have given me a dose of insanity. Let me use it for Your glory.

Balance

"A society that gives to one class all the opportunities for leisure, and to another class all the burdens of work, dooms both classes to spiritual sterility."
Lewis Mumford

Spirituality brings with it a new balance. To be relaxed, healthy, and alive, I need both work and leisure. I need to remember it is okay to take a day off. To sometimes stay in and relax is not a waste. Time for play is creative time!

I was not only compulsive around alcohol and people, but I was also obsessive about work. Perhaps I was a workaholic. I need to remember to HALT: Don't get too Hungry, Angry, Lonely, or Tired.

Work for me can be a form of escape. In leisure, I have the opportunity to meet with myself. Today I am free to enjoy myself!

You who made me a laborer in the vineyard also expected me to sit and enjoy the fruit.

Change

"It is not necessary to get away from human nature but to alter its inner attitude of heart and mind."

J. F. Newton

An understanding of sobriety and serenity that has proved helpful to me is that not only am I changing but I am involved in the change. I determine the results of the change.

I can change for good or bad. I can stay sober or can drink. I can be cheerful and creative or negative and destructive. My attitude determines the results of my changing life.

Spirituality has been given to me, but it also needs to be nurtured. I need to surround myself with loving and honest people if I am to allow my spirituality to grow. My continued willingness is essential to my sobriety and serenity.

Thank You for making me with a mind and heart that together create action.

About the Author

Leo Booth, a former Episcopal Priest, is a Unity Minister; he is also a recovering alcoholic. At the end of many years of heavy drinking, he got into a horrific car crash. That moment made him realize that life is too important to waste and so he checked himself into a treatment center.

Leo was born in England and came to America in 1981. Because of his personal experience about the dangers of alcohol and drug abuse, he dedicated his work toward recovery. His passion for helping other recovering alcoholics and drug addicts inspired him to write his first book called *Say Yes to Life*. This book has helped thousands of people over the years.

Leo continues his involvement with counseling alcoholics and addicts in several treatment centers. He speaks at many drug and alcohol abuse conferences, mental health organizations, correctional facilities, and at churches throughout the country. His books include *Say Yes to Your Spirit* and *Say Yes to Your Sexual Healing*.

Leo has appeared on such national television shows as *Oprah, Good Morning America,* and others. His articles appear in several recovery and health publications.

For more information about Leo Booth and his speaking engagements, visit: www.fatherleo.com. E-mail: fatherleo @fatherleo.com.